Counted Cross Stitch Ornaments

...and other Small Motifs

Copyright © 2022 Maggie Smith
All rights reserved. No part of this book may be reproduced or used in any manner without the prior written permission of the copyright owner, except for the use of brief quotations in a book review.

Dearest Stitchers,

This book contains a large collection of Christmas Cross Stitch patterns perfectly sized for ornaments, cards, and other small projects. These charts are fast and easy to stitch. They are great for beginning stitchers. The patterns are full color and enlarged. Most are on one page for a pleasant stitching experience. Backstitch can be added to make your projects really pop. I have also included some borders and letter sets to help you customize your holiday projects.

Happy Stitching.

\- Maggie Smith

To receive a PDF free chart, please go to my site, StitchCabin.com, and click on FREE CHART.

Tips

The Fabric

Cross stitch fabric comes in different shades. You can choose between white, antique, and various others. Be sure to choose a fabric shade that compliments your design.

The Size of the Finished Project

All of the patterns in this book are measured at 14-count. You can size a project up or down by changing the count of the fabric. To calculate the design size in inches, simply divide each dimension by 14 if using an Aida 14 fabric. (This is 14 crosses per inch) For example: If a design size is 126 x 154 you would divide 126 by 14 and 154 by 14, giving you a design that is 9" x 11" in size.
A common rule of thumb is to have at least 6 inches of fabric around your design to give you ample room for framing and matting. Be sure to factor that in when choosing your size of the fabric.

The Floss

Each pattern comes with a floss list. I use a fairly common floss, DMC. Each color lists the exact number of crosses that are required to complete the design.
The amount of floss you use can vary from stitcher to stitcher based on how tight or loose you stitch. You can use this formula:
Stitches per Skein = 17 * (15 / (6/count)) * (6/ Strands Used)
Please note that this is an approximation. There are also many online calculators to help with this.
Much Easier.

Finishing your Project

While this book focuses on the patterns themselves, here are a few ideas for finishing your ornaments:

<u>Finishing Options</u>

- Padded and backed with fabric with a lace or cordage border either glued or stitched on.
- Glued or stitched around a round ball ornament.
- Folded and stuffed into a little pillow shape, finished with decorative ribbon.
- Layered over a piece of cardboard and stitched snug in the back.
- Sewed into a satchel and stuffed with spiced herbs.
- Cut and glued on to stiff felt, finished with a hanging ribbon.
- Cut to size, and mounted over thin cardboard, and hemmed with a whipstitch.
- Cut to a rectangle and glued to a gift tag.

... and many more. Google is your friend.

Tips

*"Stitchery Tape" can be used instead of glue.
*You can stuff, to increase volume, with holiday "smell goods" like crushed cinnamon sticks.

When I'm looking to get finishing ideas, I always check YouTube. I'm very much a visual person and seeing someone make one live really helps me visualize the process.

Table of Contents

Bobbles and Things

1

9

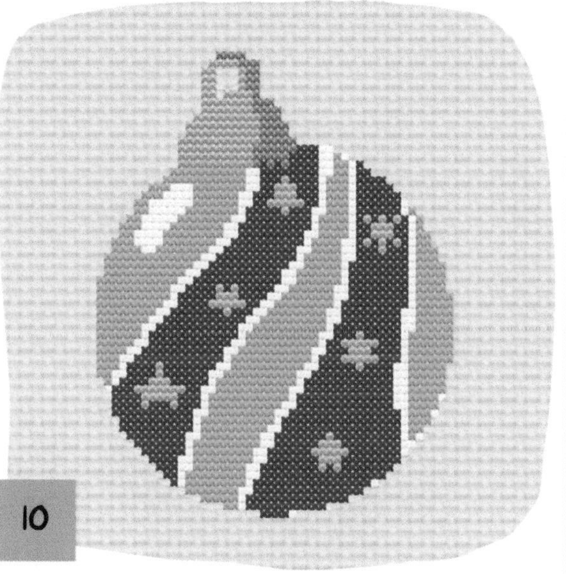
10

Table of Contents

Bobbles and Things continued...

Christmas Characters

19

20

23

Table of Contents

Christmas Characters Continued...

24

30

34

Table of Contents

Christmas Characters Continued...

Trees and Greenery

42

Table of Contents

Festive Sayings

Reindeer Games

Table of Contents

Reindeer Games Continued...

Snow Globes

58

60

64

Table of Contents

Snow Globes Continued...

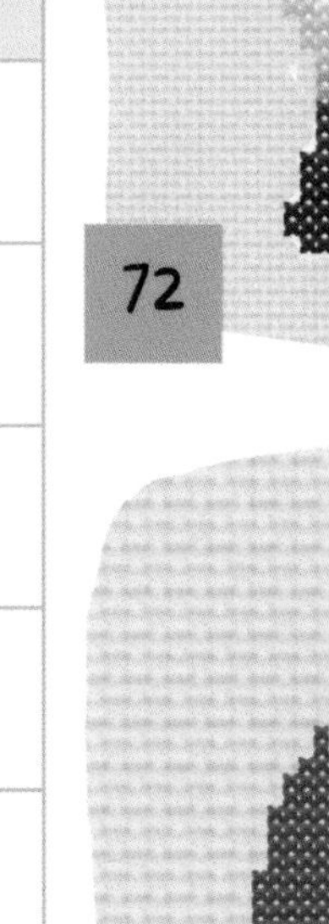

Holiday Sweets

72

80

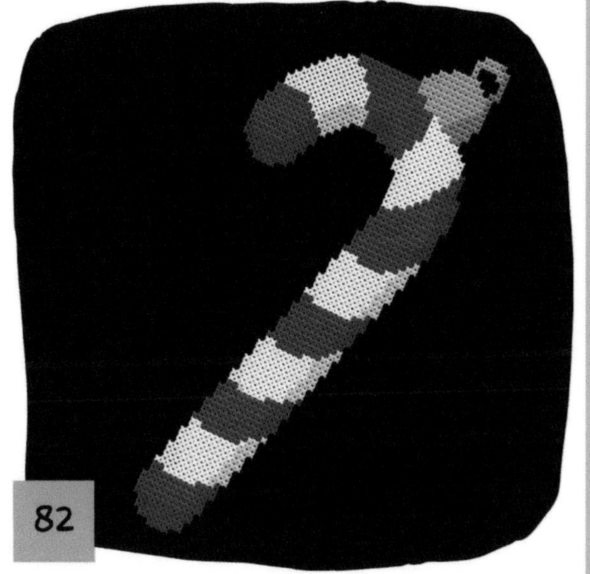

82

Table of Contents

Letters and Numbers

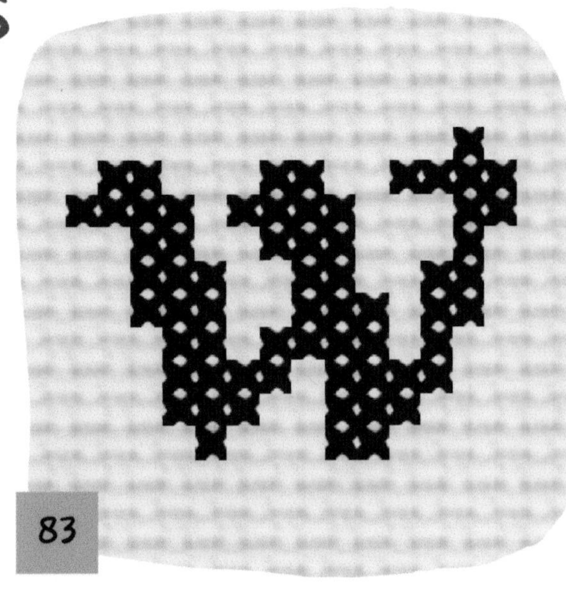

83

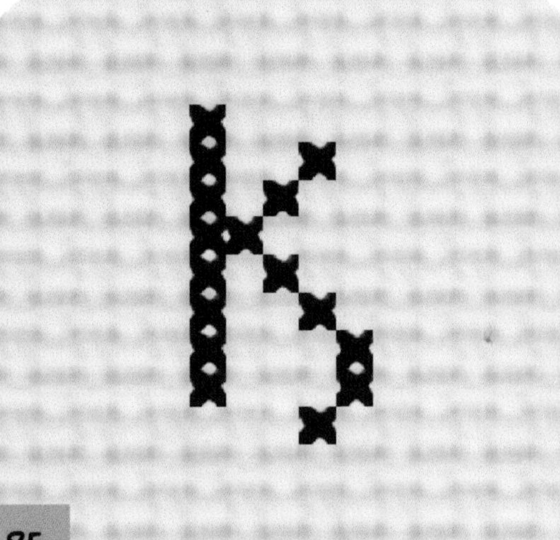

85

Snowflakes

88

~ = Size is approximate.

Table of Contents

Samplers

91

Borders

96

97

Gingerbread House

Design size: 31 x 30 stitches

Use 2 strands of thread for cross stitch

N	Symbol	Number	Name	Stitches
1	□	DMC BLANK	White	39
2	◺	DMC 919	Red Copper	19
3	∘	DMC 972	Canary - Deep	30
4	☆	DMC 976	Golden Brown - Medium	190
5	=	DMC B5200	Snow White	120
6	(	DMC 524	Fern Green - Very Light	14
7	×	DMC 747	Sky Blue - Very Light	21
8	%	DMC 817	Coral Red - Very Dark	117
9	//	DMC 905	Parrot Green - Dark	7
10	S	DMC 906	Parrot Green - Medium	4
11	⌜	DMC 3753	Antique Blue - Ultra Very Light	2
12	○	DMC 3801	Melon - Very Dark	6
13	⧗	DMC 3844	Bright Turquoise - Dark	3
14	♥	DMC 3845	Bright Turquoise - Medium	5

Use 1 strand of thread for backstitch

N	Line style	Number	Name	Units
1	——	DMC 817	Coral Red - Very Dark	124
2	——	DMC 838	Beige Brown - Very Dark	49

©2022 Maggie Smith

House with Icicles

Design size:
39 x 40 stitches

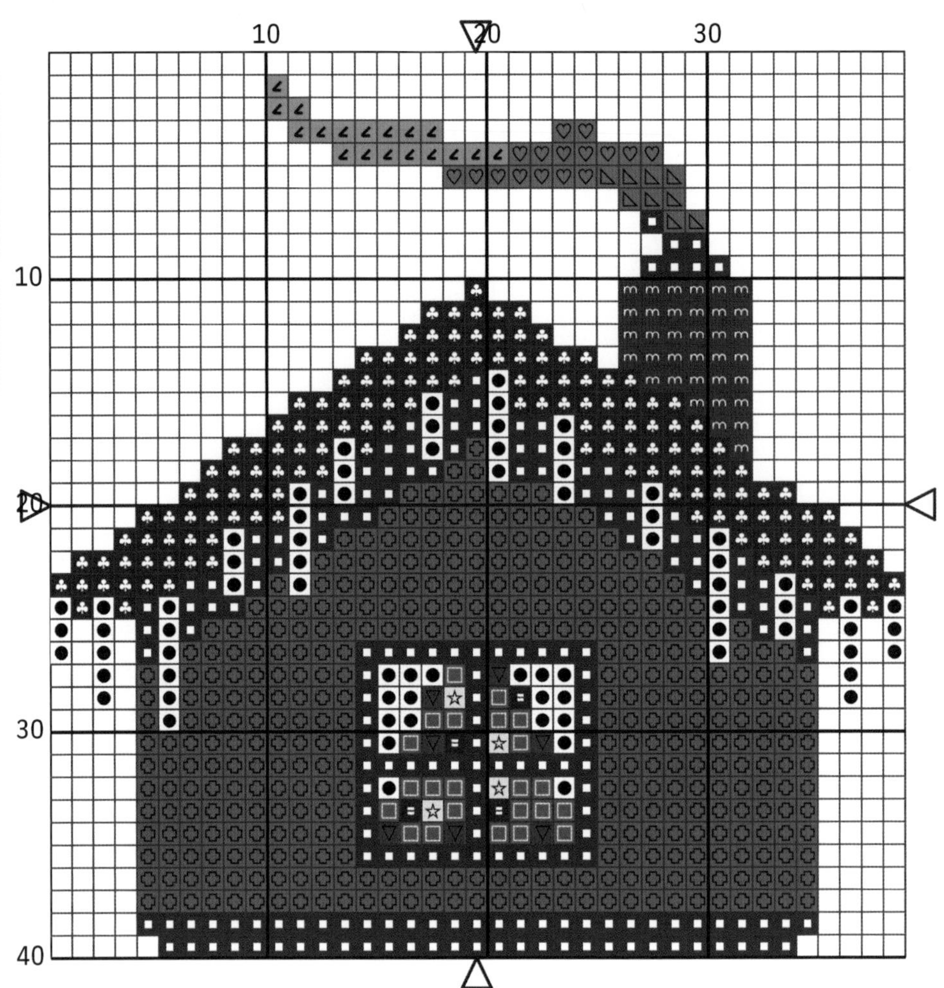

N	Symbol		Number	Name	Stitches
1	□		DMC 904	Parrot Green - Very Dark	23
2	●	●	DMC B5200	Snow White	75
3	∠	∠	DMC 318	Steel Gray - Light	18
4	♡	♡	DMC 317	Pewter Gray	16
5	◺	◺	DMC 04	Tin - Dark	9
6	♣	♣	DMC 898	Coffee Brown - Very Dark	151
7	m	m	DMC 919	Red Copper	35
8	✚	✚	DMC 3787	Brown Gray - Dark	367
9	■	□	DMC 09	Cocoa - Very Dark	184
10	▽	▽	DMC 321	Red	7
11	☆	☆	DMC 12	Tender Green	4
12	=	=	DMC 550	Violet - Very Dark	4

Use 2 strands of thread for cross stitch

©2022 Maggie Smith

House with Lights

Design size:
39 x 40 stitches

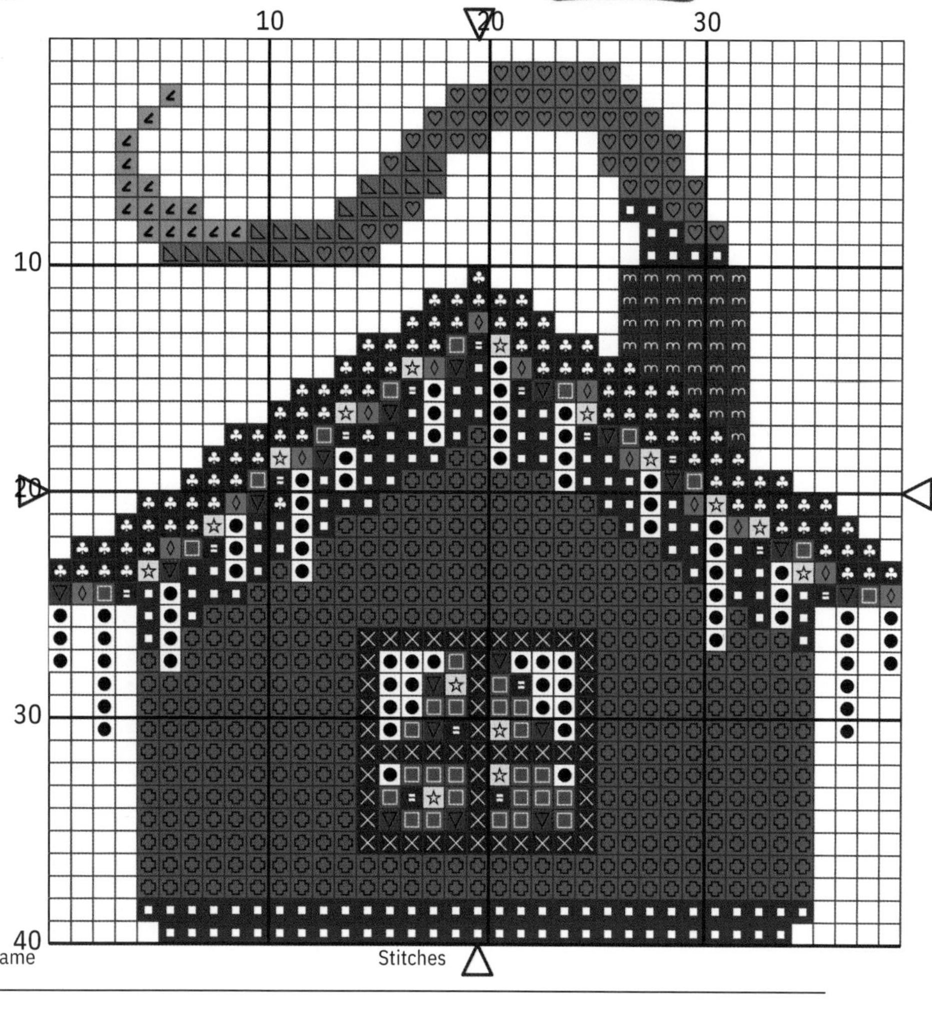

N	Symbol	Number	Name	Stitches
1	□	DMC 904	Parrot Green - Very Dark	34
2	●	DMC B5200	Snow White	74
3	◺	DMC 04	Tin - Dark	21
4	■	DMC 09	Cocoa - Very Dark	131
5	☆	DMC 12	Tender Green	15
6	♡	DMC 317	Pewter Gray	53
7	∠	DMC 318	Steel Gray - Light	15
8	▽	DMC 321	Red	18
9	=	DMC 550	Violet - Very Dark	15
10	♣	DMC 898	Coffee Brown - Very Dark	98
11	✕	DMC 898	Coffee Brown - Very Dark	54
12	m	DMC 919	Red Copper	35
13	✚	DMC 3787	Brown Gray - Dark	369
14	◊	DMC 3843	Electric Blue	14

Use 2 strands of thread for cross stitch

©2022 Maggie Smith

Red Stocking

Design size:
29 x 40 stitches

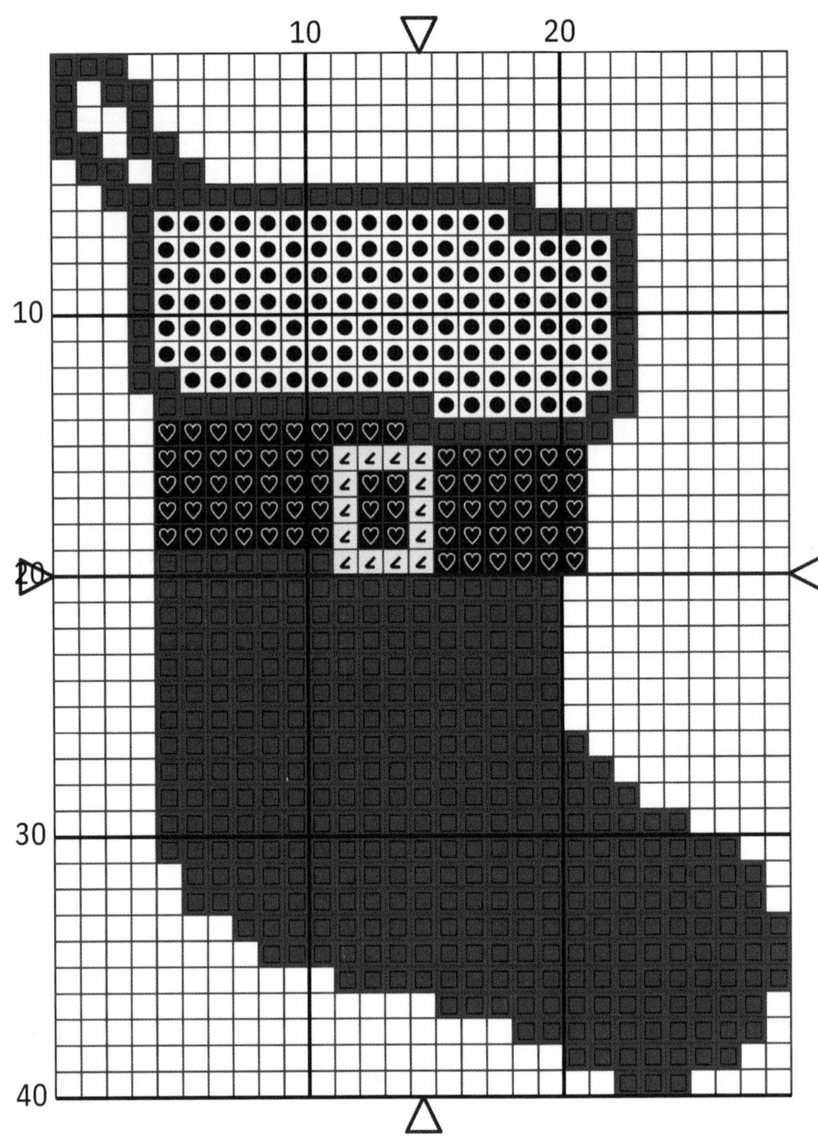

Use 2 strands of thread for cross stitch

N	Symbol		Number	Name	Stitches
1	□	■	DMC 666	Red - Bright	414
2	●	●	DMC B5200	Snow White	127
3	∠	∠	DMC 307	Lemon	14
4	♡	♡	DMC 310	Black	74

©2022 Maggie Smith

Red and Green Stocking with Snowflake

Design size: 29 x 40 stitches

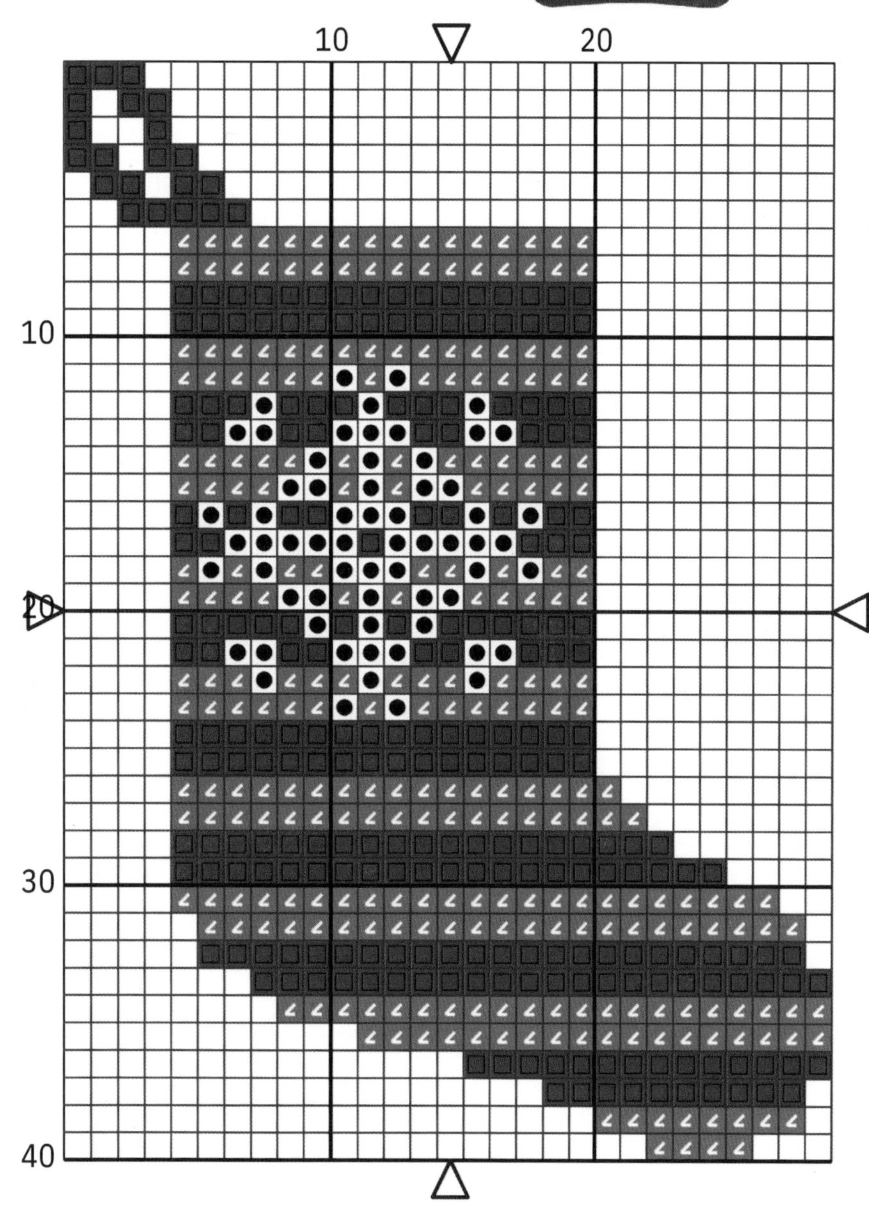

Use 2 strands of thread for cross stitch

N	Symbol		Number	Name	Stitches
1	□	■	DMC 666	Red - Bright	253
2	●	●	DMC B5200	Snow White	64
3	∠	∠	DMC 905	Parrot Green - Dark	265

©2022 Maggie Smith

Candle

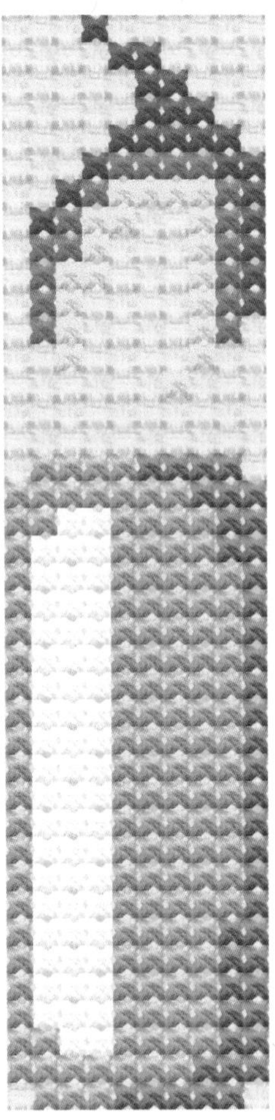

Design size: 10 x 40 stitches

Use 2 strands of thread for cross stitch

N	Symbol		Number	Name	Stitches
1	□	□	DMC 738	Tan - Very Light	136
2	●	●	DMC B5200	Snow White	58
3	∠	∠	DMC 307	Lemon	19
4	♡	♡	DMC 740	Tangerine	17
5	◺	◺	DMC 946	Burnt Orange - Medium	23
6	♣	♣	DMC 3064	Desert Sand	42

©2022 Maggie Smith

Christmas Gift

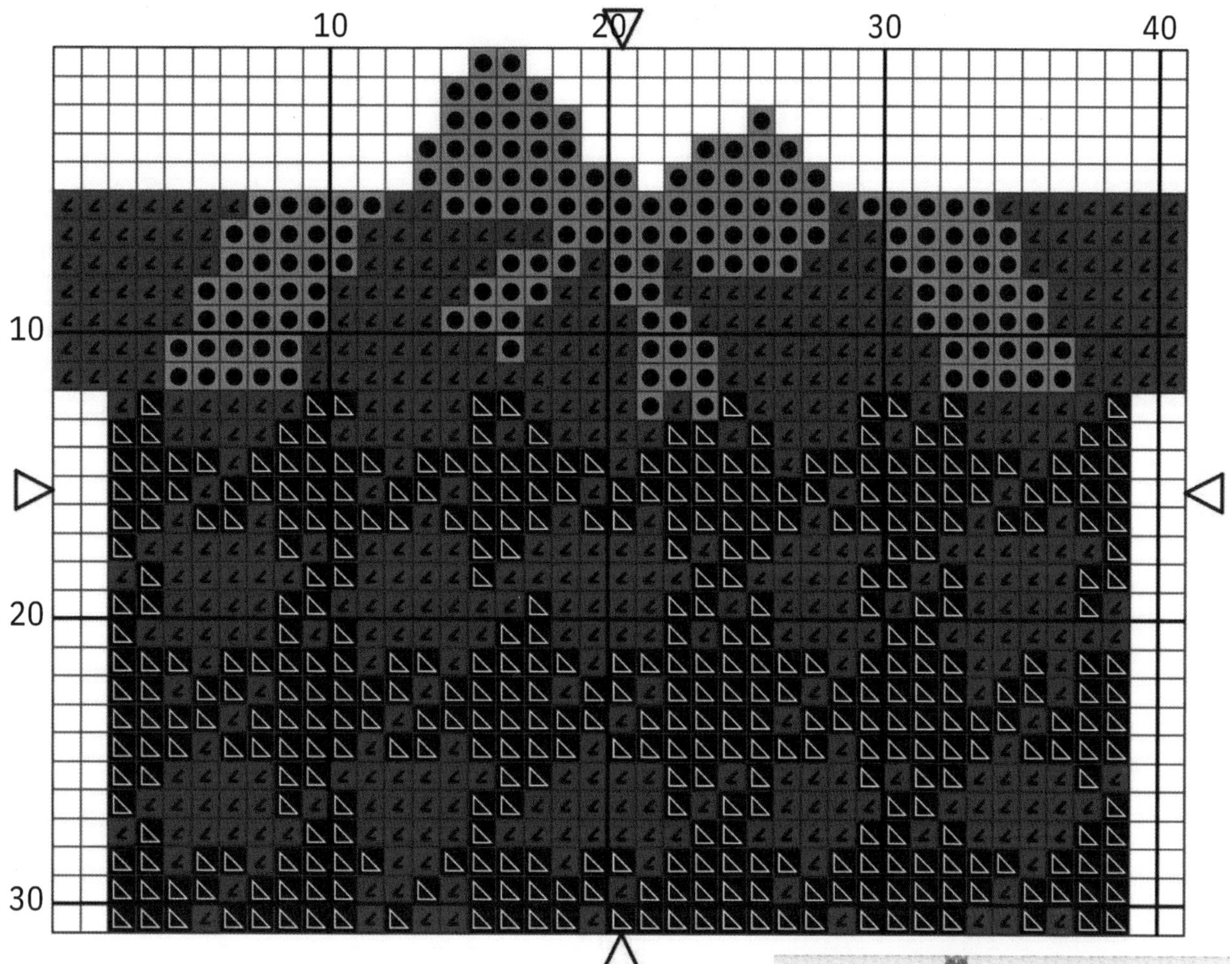

Design size: 41 x 31 stitches

Use 2 strands of thread for cross stitch

N	Symbol	Number	Name	Stitches
1	◺	DMC 310	Black	403
2	∠	DMC 321	Red	465
3	●	DMC 680	Old Gold - Dark	158

©2022 Maggie Smith

Gift

Design size: 46 x 56 stitches

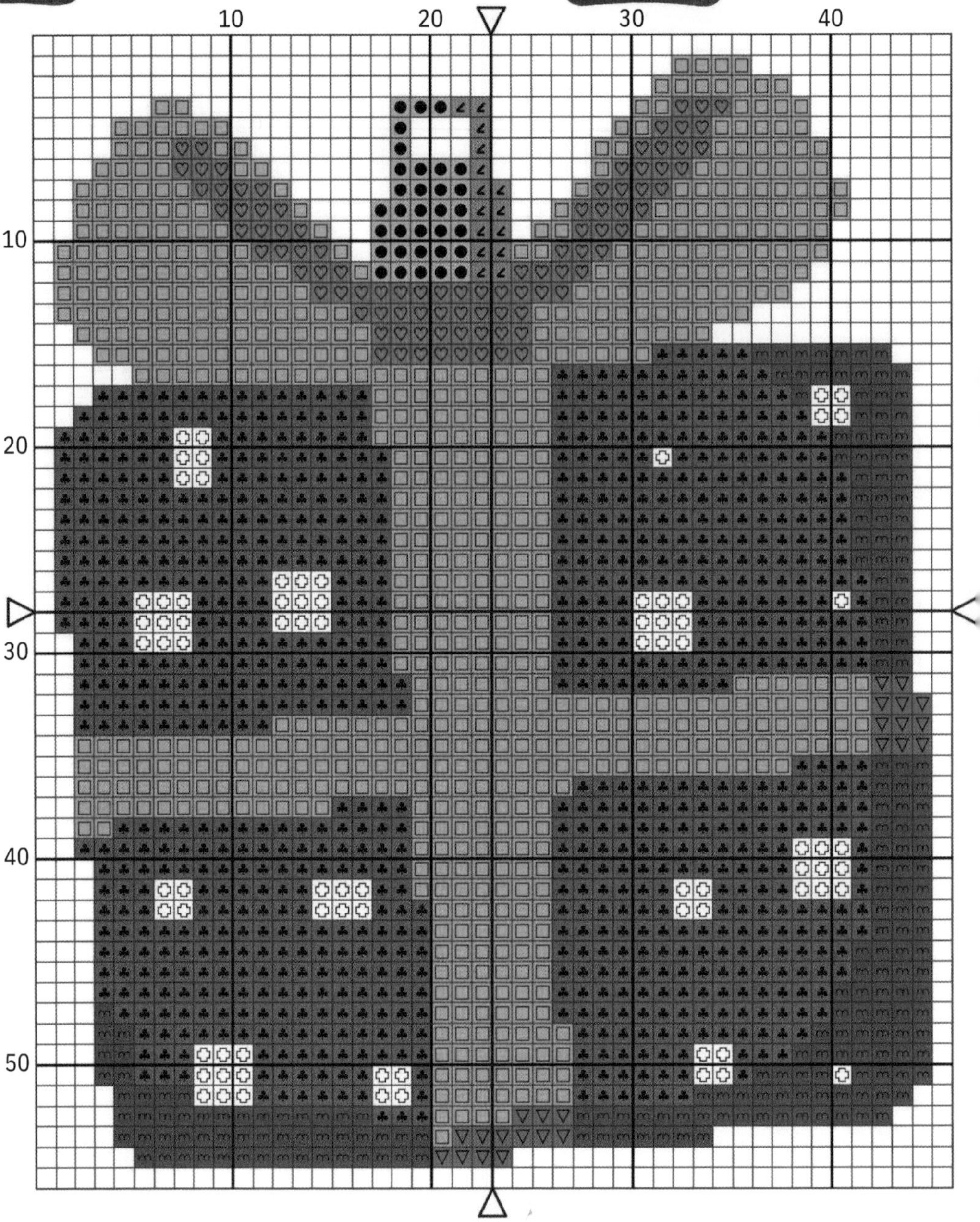

N	Symbol	Number	Name	Stitches
1	m	DMC 350	Coral - Medium	209
2	∠	DMC 680	Old Gold - Dark	15
3	●	DMC 972	Canary - Deep	33
4	♣	DMC 3705	Melon - Dark	888
5	□	DMC 3845	Bright Turquoise - Medium	681
6	♡	DMC 3850	Bright Green - Dark	94
7	✚	DMC B5200	Snow White	80
8	▽	DMC 3768	Gray Green - Dark	24

Use 2 strands of thread for cross stitch

©2022 Maggie Smith

Bell

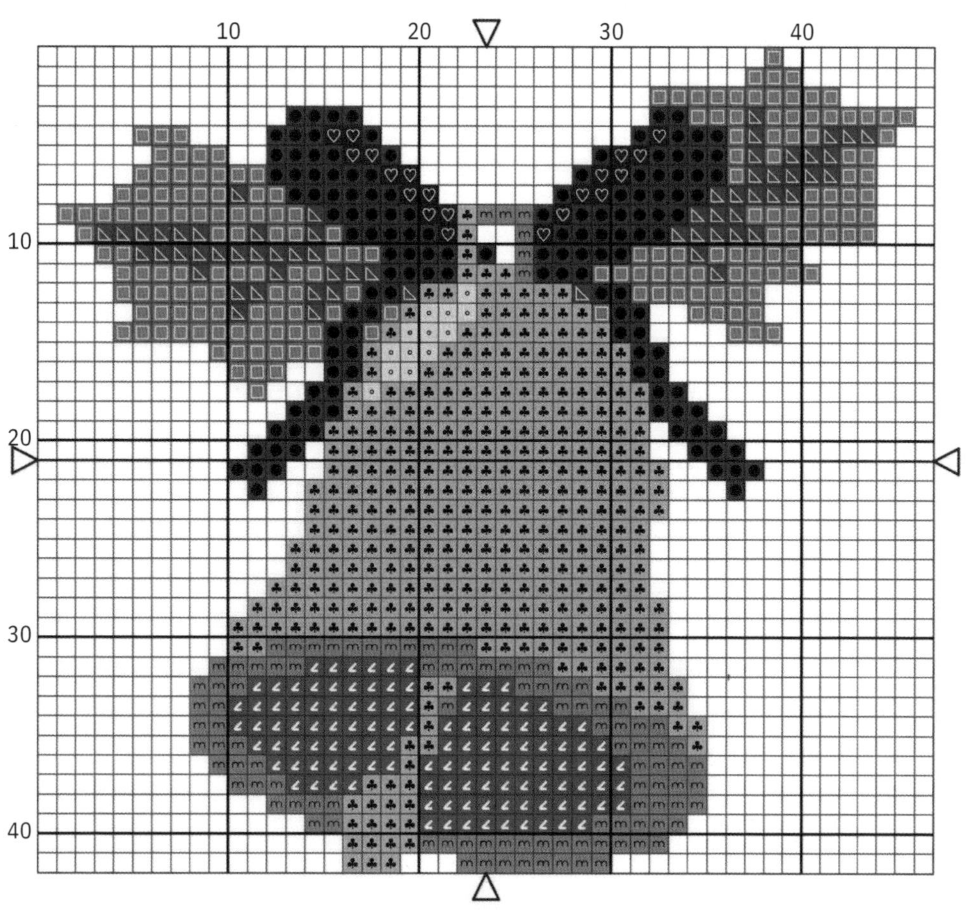

Design size: 47 x 42 stitches

Use 2 strands of thread for cross stitch

N	Symbol		Number	Name	Stitches
1	m	m	DMC 680	Old Gold - Dark	106
2	◺	◺	DMC 699	Green	62
3	♡	♡	DMC 814	Garnet - Dark	20
4	●	●	DMC 817	Coral Red - Very Dark	138
5	∠	∠	DMC 829	Golden Olive - Very Dark	121
6	□	□	DMC 910	Emerald Green - Dark	184
7	♣	♣	DMC 972	Canary - Deep	348
8	∘	∘	DMC 973	Canary - Bright	13

©2022 Maggie Smith

Ball Ornament

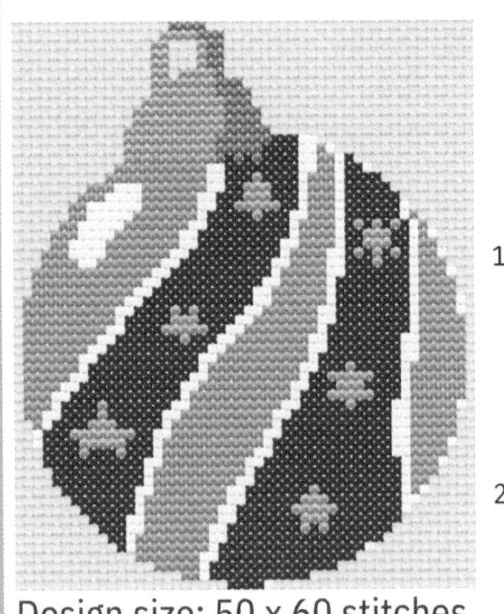

Design size: 50 x 60 stitches

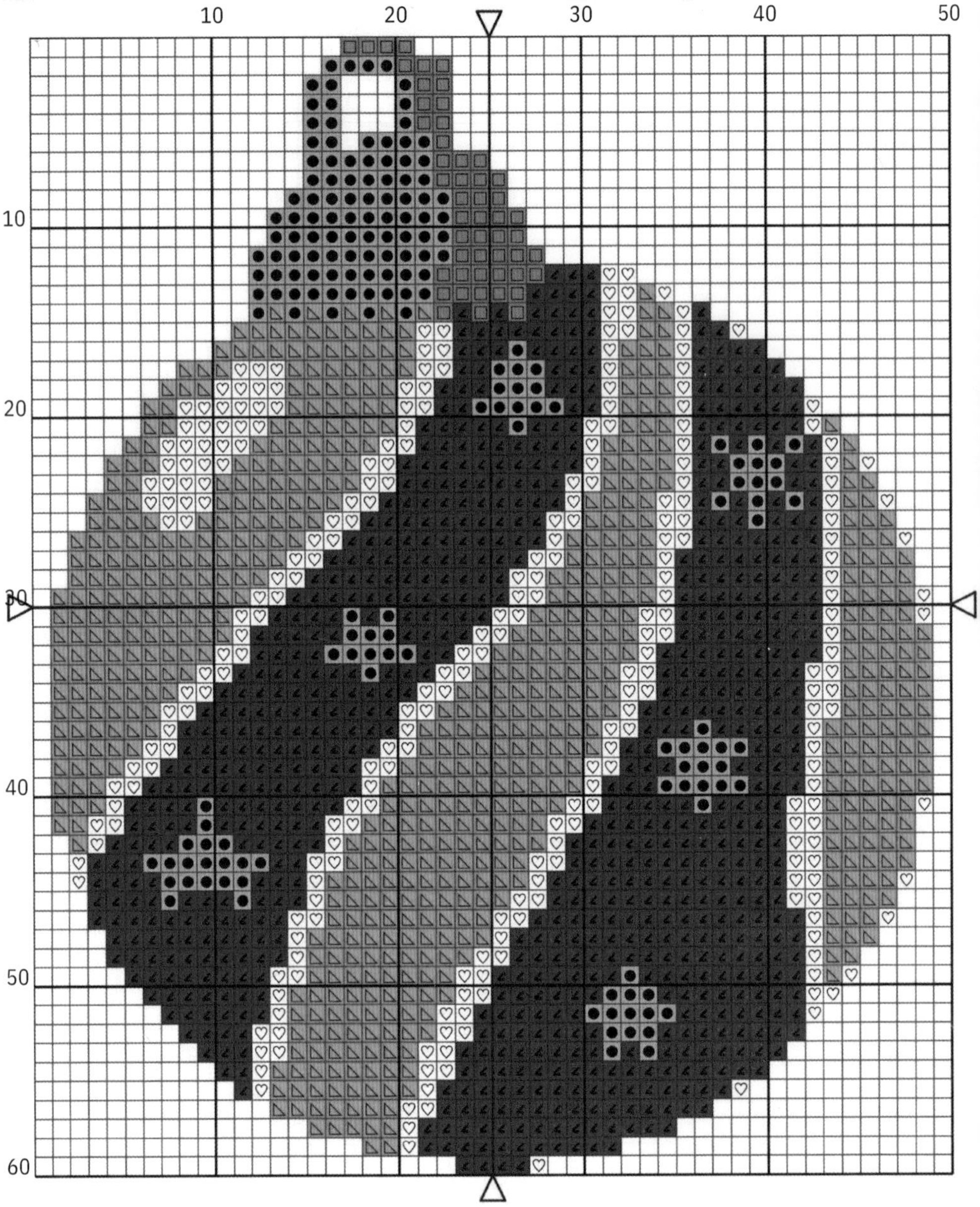

Use 2 strands of thread for cross stitch

N	Symbol	Number	Name	Stitches
1		DMC 321	Red	788
2	□	DMC 680	Old Gold - Dark	51
3	●	DMC 728	Golden Yellow	183
4	♡	DMC B5200	Snow White	282
5	◺	DMC 906	Parrot Green - Medium	659

©2022 Maggie Smith

Teardrop Ornament

Design size: 43 x 75 stitches

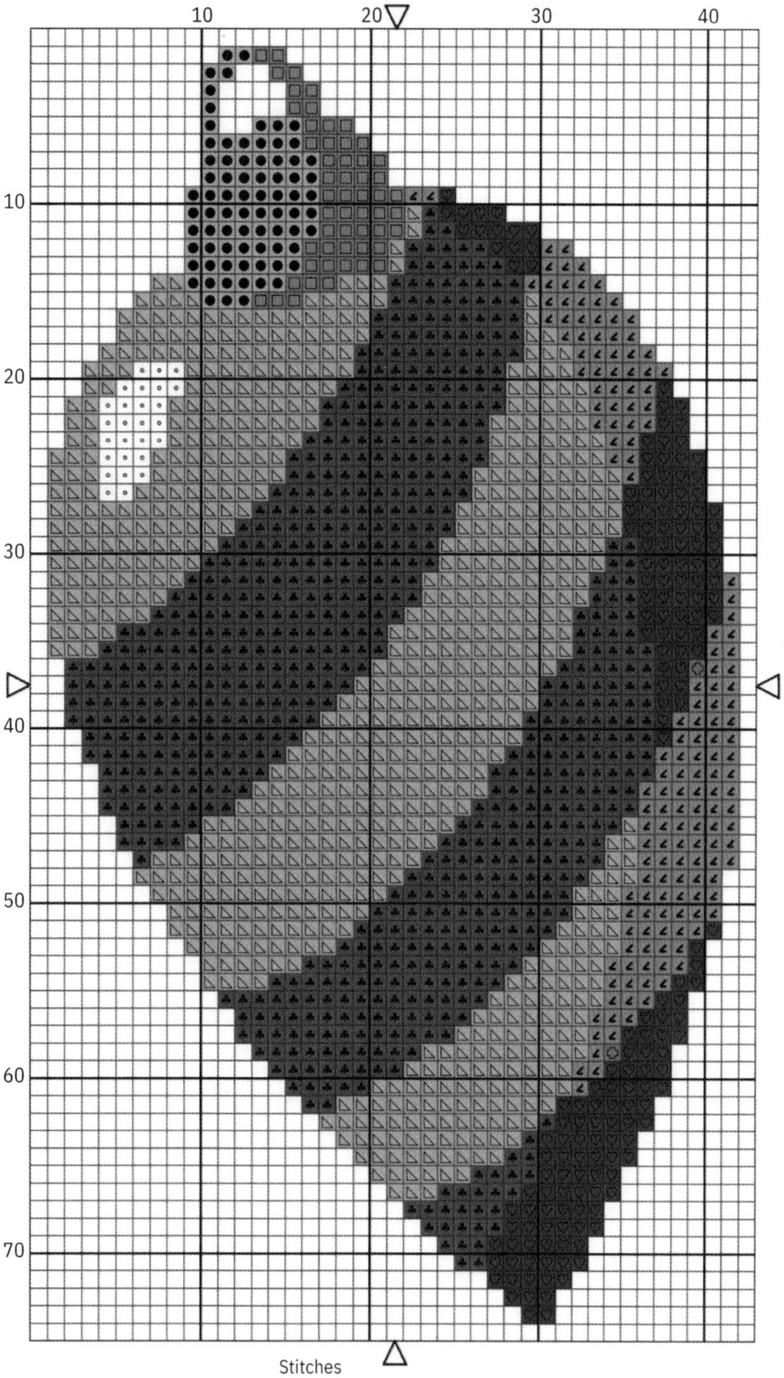

N	Symbol	Number	Name	Stitches
1	♡	DMC 326	Rose - Very Dark	183
2	□	DMC 680	Old Gold - Dark	54
3	●	DMC 972	Canary - Deep	77
4	♣	DMC 3801	Melon - Very Dark	711
5	∠	DMC 3812	Seagreen - Very Dark	166
6	°	DMC 3845	Bright Turquoise - Medium	747
7	◺	DMC B5200	Snow White	27

Use 2 strands of thread for cross stitch

©2022 Maggie Smith

Star

Design size: 40 x 46 stitches

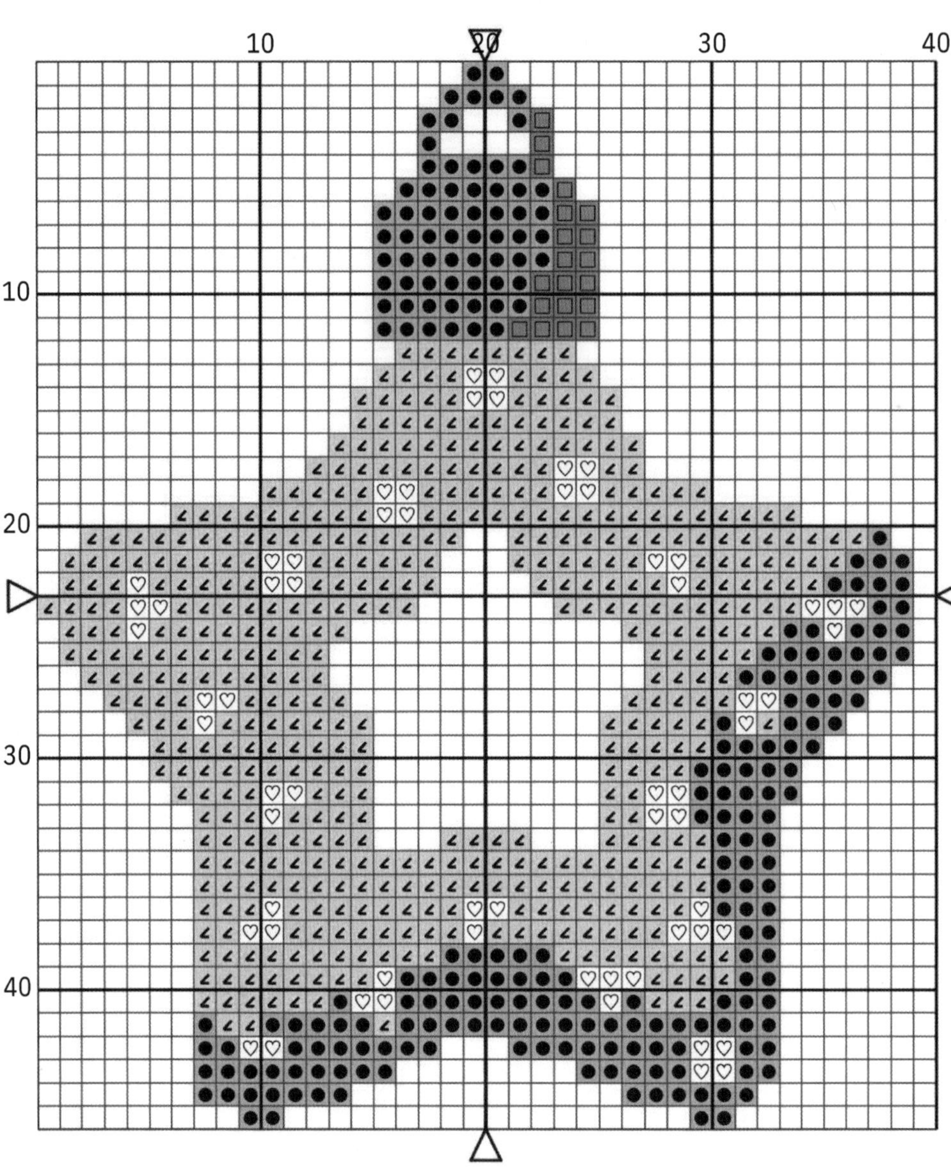

Use 2 strands of thread for cross stitch

N	Symbol		Number	Name	Stitches
1	∠	∠	DMC 444	Lemon - Dark	491
2	□	□	DMC 680	Old Gold - Dark	20
3	●	●	DMC 972	Canary - Deep	242
4	♡	♡	DMC B5200	Snow White	63

©2022 Maggie Smith

Bell and Pink Bow

Design size:
35 x 40 stitches

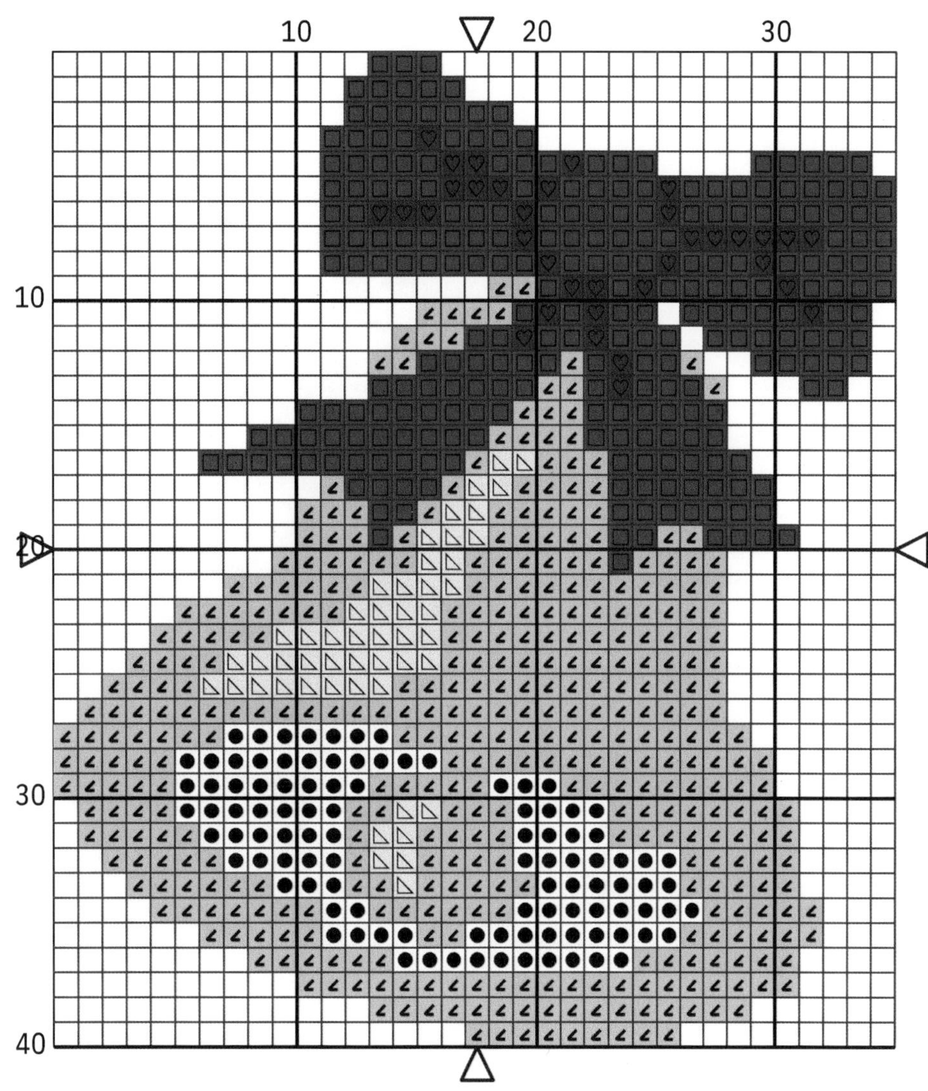

Use 2 strands of thread for cross stitch

N	Symbol		Number	Name	Stitches
1	□	▣	DMC 600	Cranberry - Very Dark	254
2	●	●	DMC B5200	Snow White	104
3	♡	♡	DMC 326	Rose - Very Dark	35
4	∠	∠	DMC 743	Yellow - Medium	401
5	◺	◺	DMC 3889	Lemon - Medium Light	50

©2022 Maggie Smith

Bell and Red Bow

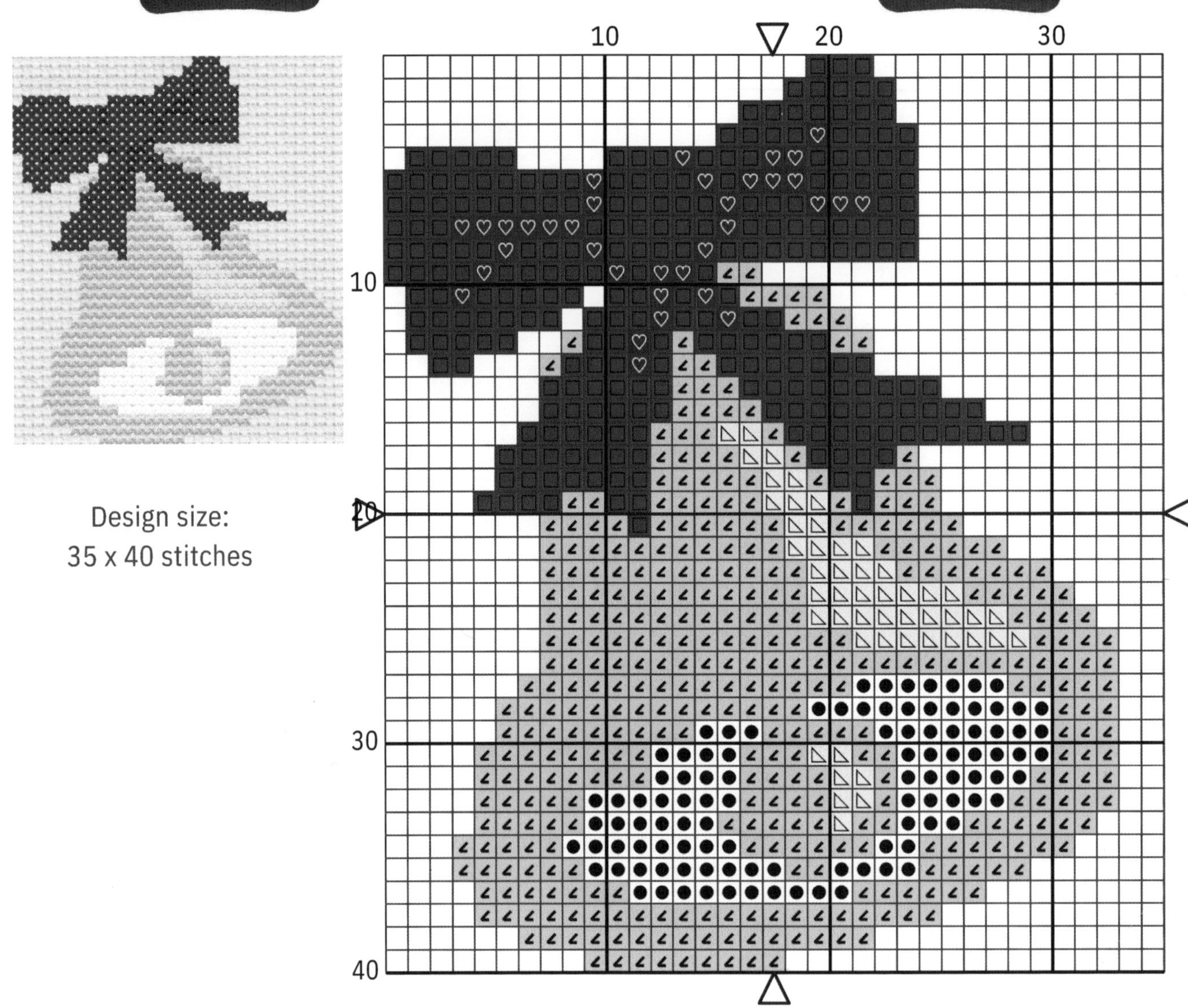

Design size:
35 x 40 stitches

Use 2 strands of thread for cross stitch

N	Symbol		Number	Name	Stitches
1	□	□	DMC 666	Red - Bright	254
2	●	●	DMC B5200	Snow White	104
3	∠	∠	DMC 743	Yellow - Medium	401
4	♡	♡	DMC 919	Red Copper	35
5	◺	◺	DMC 3889	Lemon - Medium Light	50

©2022 Maggie Smith

Red Ball Ornament

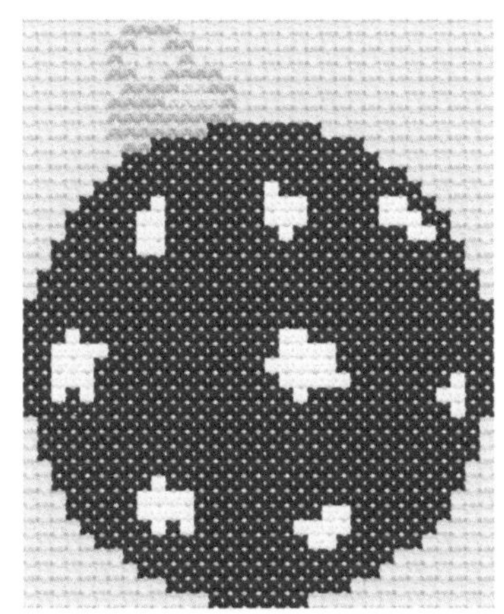

Design size:
33 x 40 stitches

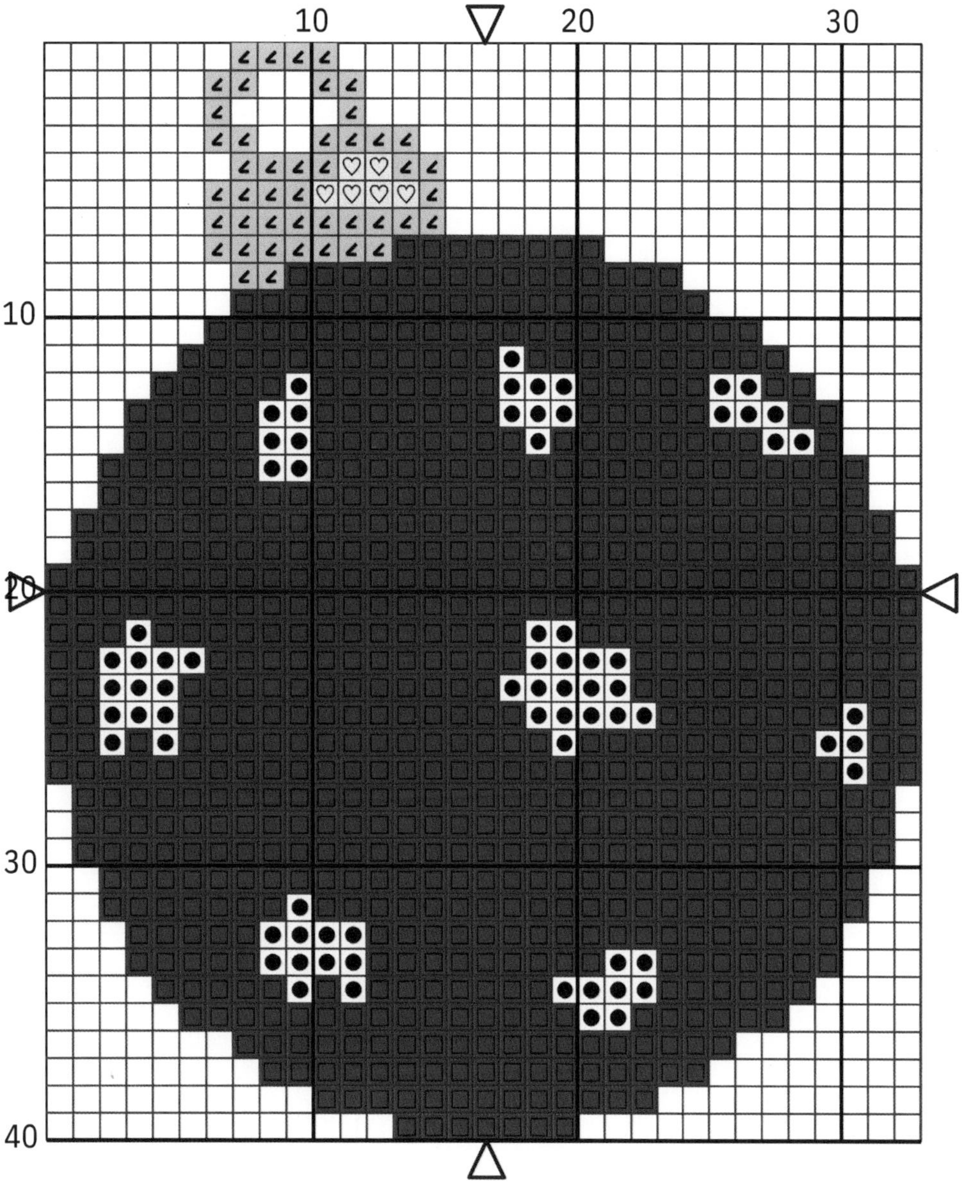

Use 2 strands of thread for cross stitch

N	Symbol		Number	Name	Stitches
1	□	■	DMC 321	Red	782
2	●	●	DMC B5200	Snow White	75
3	∠	∠	DMC 743	Yellow - Medium	45
4	♡	♡	DMC 3889	Lemon - Medium Light	6

©2022 Maggie Smith

Green Ball Ornament with Snowflake

Design size:
33 x 40 stitches

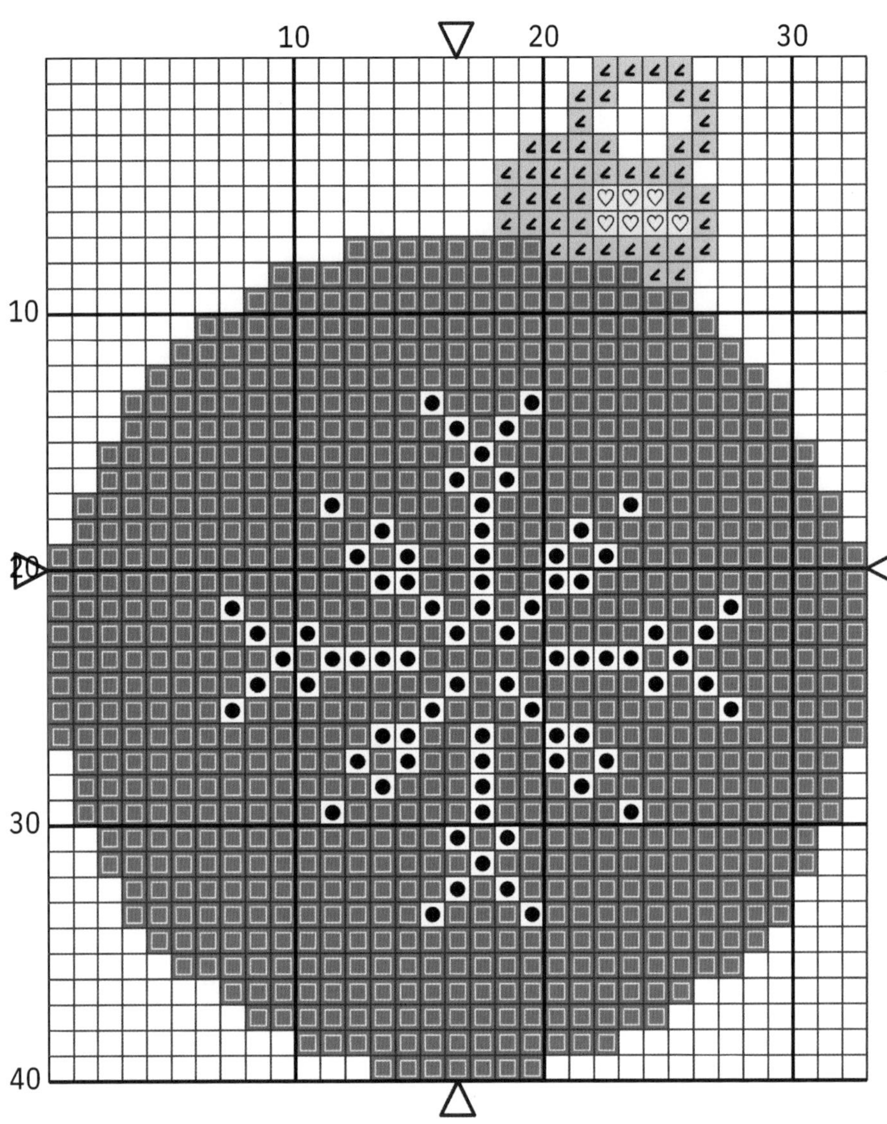

Use 2 strands of thread for cross stitch

N	Symbol		Number	Name	Stitches
1	□	□	DMC 905	Parrot Green - Dark	780
2	●	●	DMC B5200	Snow White	77
3	∠	∠	DMC 743	Yellow - Medium	44
4	♡	♡	DMC 3889	Lemon - Medium Light	7

©2022 Maggie Smith

Blue Angel

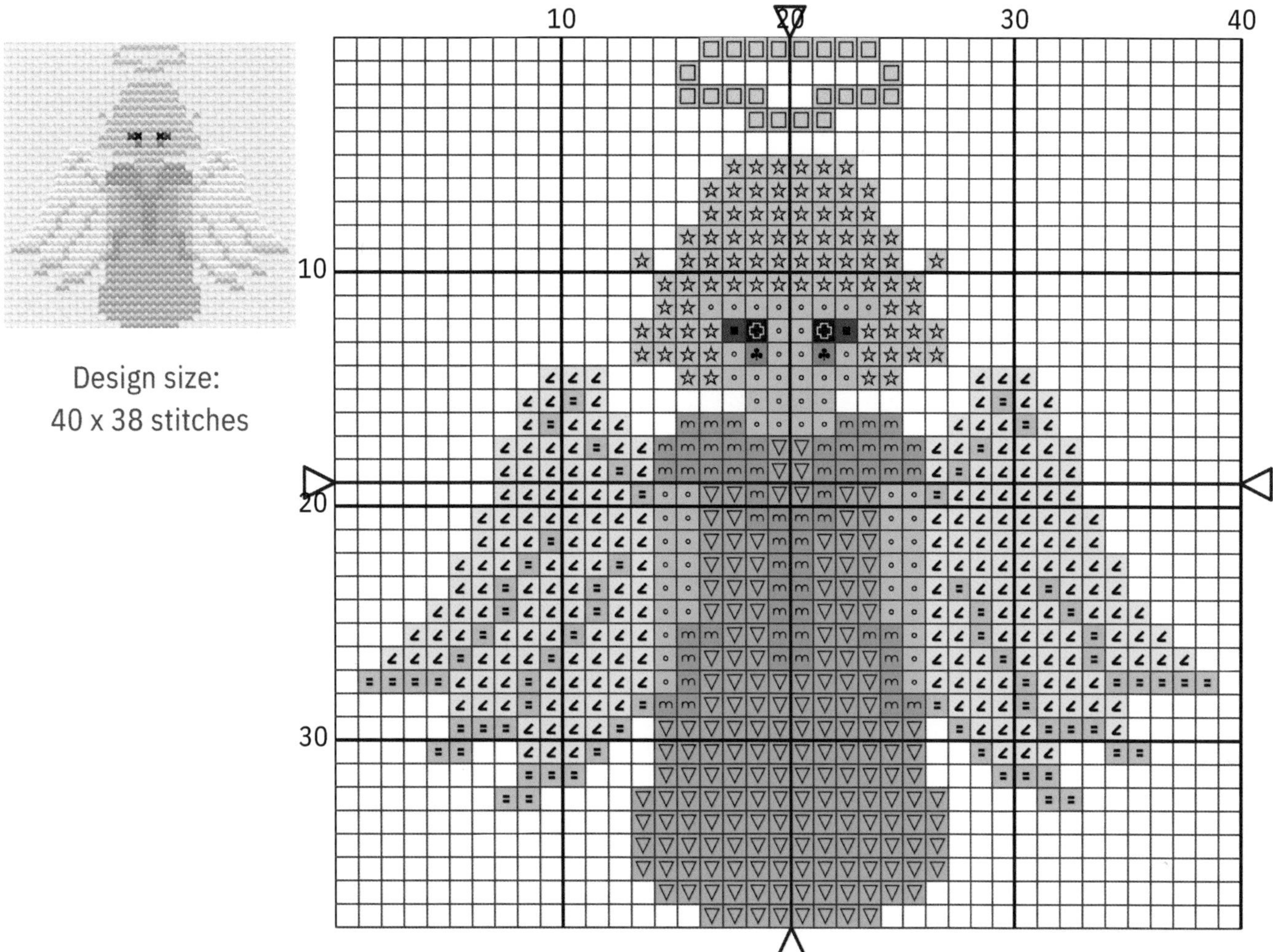

Design size:
40 x 38 stitches

Use 2 strands of thread for cross stitch

N	Symbol	Number	Name	Stitches
1	=	DMC 01	Tin - White	68
2	▽	DMC 26	Lavender - Pale	176
3	m	DMC 156	Blue - Medium	56
4	□	DMC 743	Yellow - Medium	22
5	■	DMC 779	Brown	2
6	✚	DMC 3371	Black Brown	2
7	∠	DMC 3756	Baby Blue - Ultra Very Light	214
8	♣	DMC 3806	Cyclamen Pink - Light	2
9	☆	DMC 3822	Straw - Light	80
10	∘	DMC 3893	Mocha Beige - Very Light	58

©2022 Maggie Smith

Pink Angel

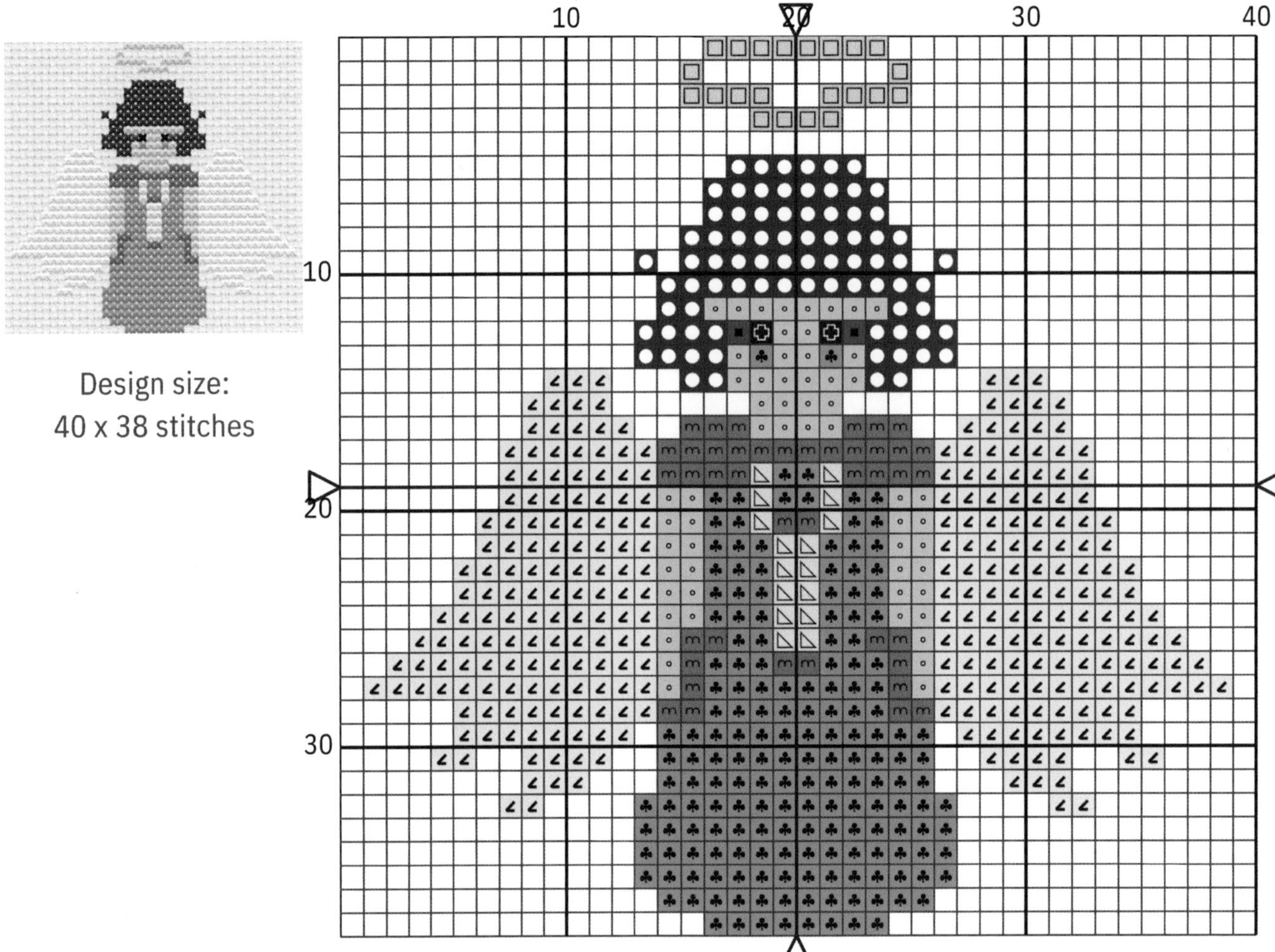

Design size:
40 x 38 stitches

Use 2 strands of thread for cross stitch

N	Symbol		Number	Name	Stitches
1	□	□	DMC 743	Yellow - Medium	22
2	■	■	DMC 779	Brown	2
3	◺	◺	DMC 818	Baby Pink	16
4	m	m	DMC 893	Carnation - Light	42
5	●	○	DMC 919	Red Copper	80
6	✚	✚	DMC 3371	Black Brown	2
7	∠	∠	DMC 3756	Baby Blue - Ultra Very Light	282
8	♣	♣	DMC 3806	Cyclamen Pink - Light	176
9	∘	∘	DMC 3893	Mocha Beige - Very Light	58

©2022 Maggie Smith

Reindeer

Design size: 22 x 28 stitches

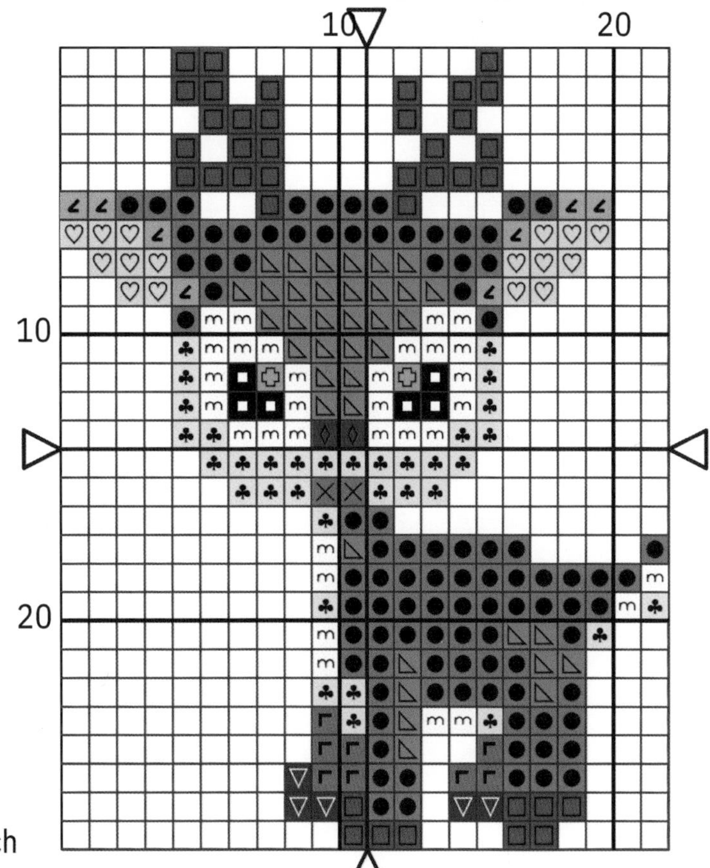

Use 2 strands of thread for cross stitch

N	Symbol		Number	Name	Stitches
1	□	□	DMC 301	Mahogany - Medium	38
2	●	●	DMC 922	Copper - Light	95
3	♡	♡	DMC 950	Desert Sand - Light	16
4	∠	∠	DMC 3825	Pumpkin - Pale	8
5	♣	♣	DMC 3866	Mocha Brown - Ultra Very Light	34
6	◺	◺	DMC 3883	Copper - Medium Light	38
7	m	m	DMC B5200	Snow White	32
8	■	■	DMC 310	Black	6
9	◊	◊	DMC 321	Red	2
10	✚	✚	DMC 648	Beaver Gray - Light	2
11	✕	✕	DMC 3712	Salmon - Medium	2
12	⌐	⌐	DMC 3776	Mahogany - Light	8
13	▽	▽	DMC 3858	Rosewood - Medium	5

©2022 Maggie Smith

Penguin

Design size: 21 x 29 stitches

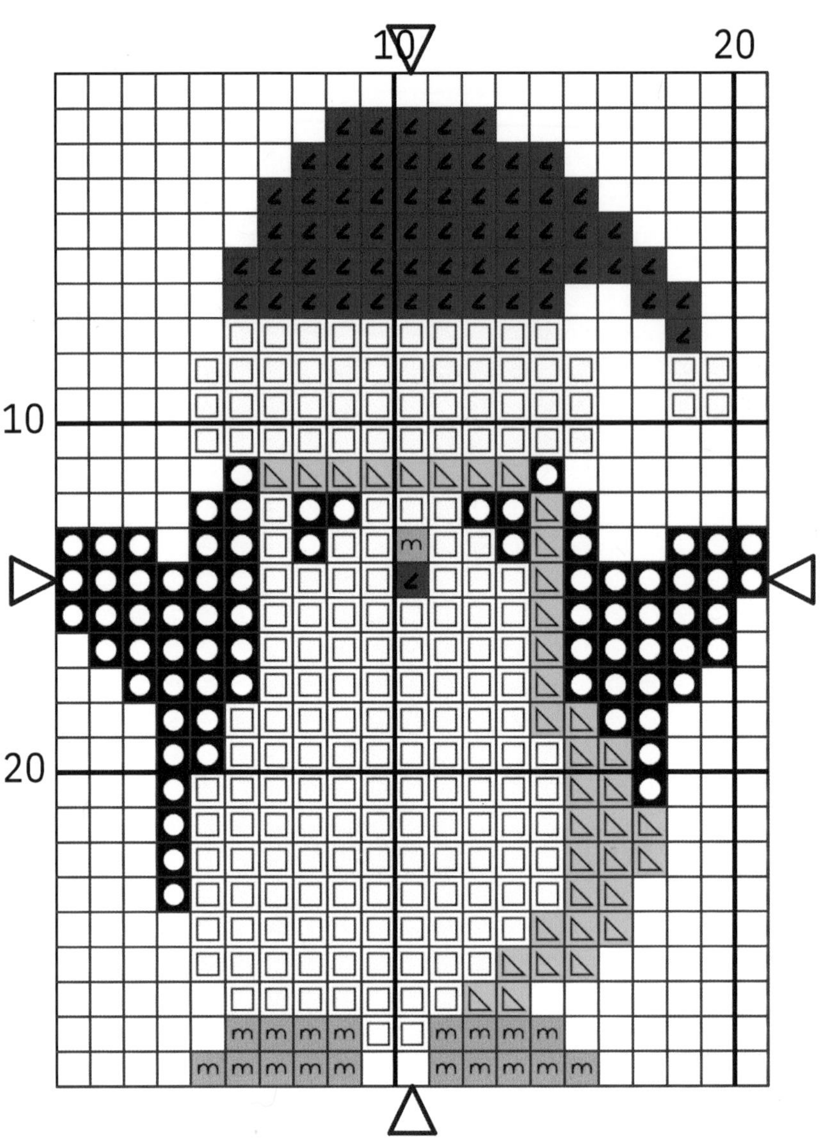

Use 2 strands of thread for cross stitch

N	Symbol		Number	Name	Stitches
1	□	□	DMC B5200	Snow White	181
2	●	○	DMC 310	Black	73
3	∠	∠	DMC 321	Red	61
4	m	m	DMC 972	Canary - Deep	19
5	◺	◺	DMC 3024	Brown Gray - Very Light	36

©2022 Maggie Smith

Winter Penguin

Design size: 55 x 90 stitches

Use 2 strands of thread for cross stitch

N	Symbol	Number	Name	Stitches
1	♣	DMC 221	Shell Pink - Very Dark	165
2	m	DMC 907	Parrot Green - Light	259
3	∘	DMC B5200	Snow White	635
4	✚	DMC 15	Apple Green	151
5	▽	DMC 310	Black	753
6	┏	DMC 740	Tangerine	141
7	=	DMC 742	Tangerine - Light	108
8	✕	DMC 817	Coral Red - Very Dark	689
9	■	DMC 3713	Salmon - Very Light	20

©2022 Maggie Smith

Winter Penguin 2

Design size: 55 x 104 stitches

Use 2 strands of thread for cross stitch

N	Symbol	Number	Name	Stitches
1	●	DMC 602	Cranberry - Medium	107
2	♡	DMC 605	Cranberry - Very Light	325
3	□	DMC 956	Geranium	584
4	∠	DMC 957	Geranium - Pale	214
5	◺	DMC 3806	Cyclamen Pink - Light	159
6	✚	DMC B5200	Snow White	1178
7	▽	DMC 310	Black	833
8	=	DMC 742	Tangerine - Light	32

©2022 Maggie Smith

Winter Penguin 3

Design size: 53 x 70 stitches

N	Symbol	Number	Name	Stitches
1	●	DMC 304	Red - Medium	162
2	□	DMC 321	Red	391
3	∠	DMC 803	Blue - Deep	76
4	♡	DMC 3807	Cornflower Blue	63
5	◺	DMC B5200	Snow White	658
6	m	DMC 156	Blue - Medium	40
7	7	DMC 310	Black	598
8	#	DMC 605	Cranberry - Very Light	19
9	┏	DMC 740	Tangerine	41
10	◊	DMC 742	Tangerine - Light	108

Use 2 strands of thread for cross stitch

©2022 Maggie Smith

Winter Penguin 4

Design size: 54 x 77 stitches

N	Symbol		Number	Name	Stitches
1	●	○	DMC 310	Black	610
2	□	▣	DMC 816	Garnet	314
3	∠	∠	DMC 3812	Seagreen - Very Dark	464
4	♡	♡	DMC B5200	Snow White	690
5	▽	▽	DMC 351	Coral	314
6	m	m	DMC 725	Topaz	34
7	◺	◺	DMC 747	Sky Blue - Very Light	462
	∘	∘	DMC 963	Dusty Rose - Ultra Very Light	20

Use 2 strands of thread for cross stitch

©2022 Maggie Smith

Gnome

Design size: 25 x 26 stitches

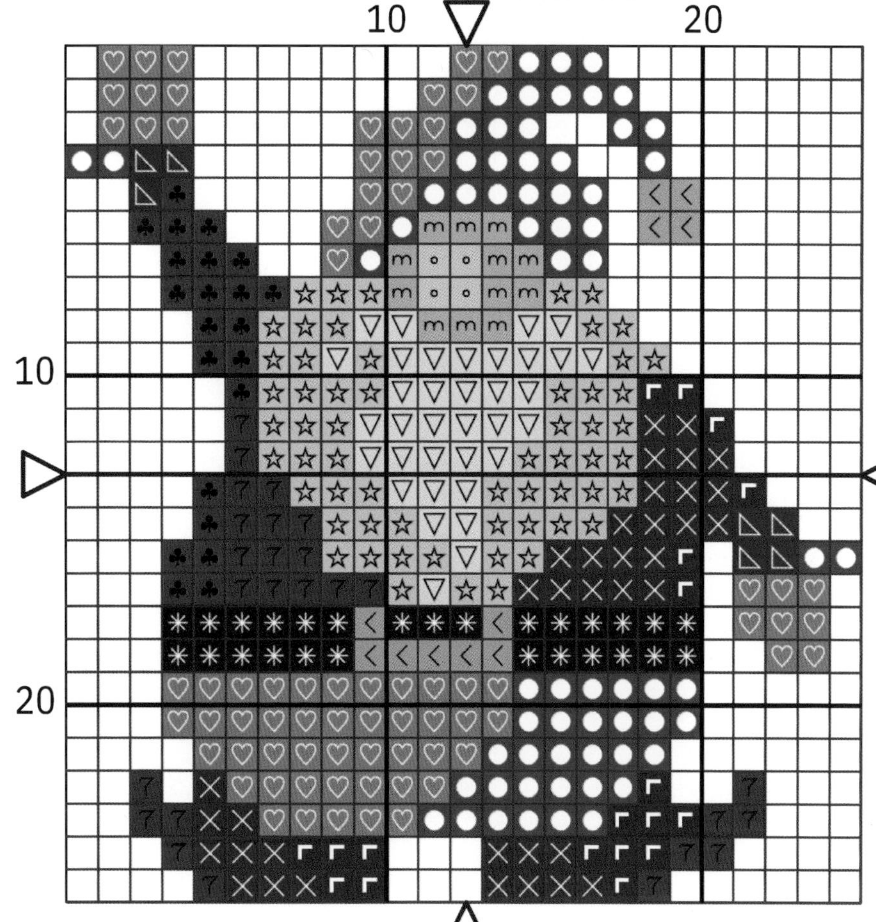

Use 2 strands of thread for cross stitch

N	Symbol	Number	Name	Stitches
1	7	DMC 326	Rose - Very Dark	26
2	♡	DMC 701	Green - Light	75
3	▽	DMC 762	Pearl Gray - Very Light	35
4	┏	DMC 777	Red - Deep	19
5	✕	DMC 816	Garnet	37
6	♣	DMC 817	Coral Red - Very Dark	22
7	◺	DMC 820	Royal Blue - Very Dark	7
8	∘	DMC 967	Peach - Light	4
9	☆	DMC 3024	Brown Gray - Very Light	59
10	✳	DMC 3371	Black Brown	27
11	●	DMC 3818	Emerald Green - Ultra Very Dark	65
12	m	DMC 3824	Apricot - Light	12
13	<	DMC 3854	Autumn Gold - Medium	11

©2022 Maggie Smith

Santa

Design size: 43 x 59 stitches

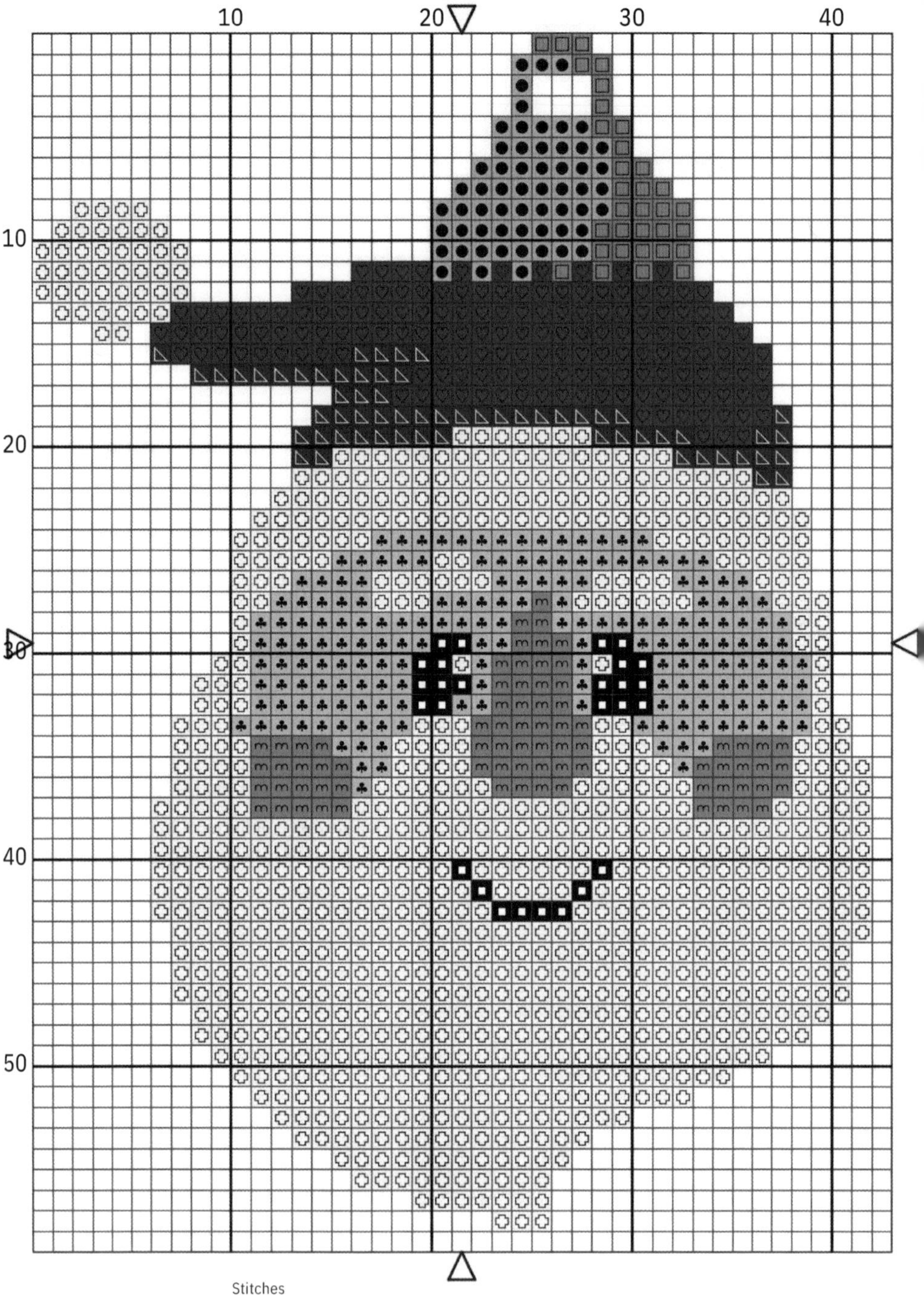

N	Symbol	Number	Name	Stitches
1	♡	DMC 321	Red	162
2	□	DMC 680	Old Gold - Dark	33
3	◺	DMC 816	Garnet	61
4	●	DMC 972	Canary - Deep	59
5	m	DMC 3778	Terra Cotta - Light	77
6	♣	DMC 3856	Mahogany - Ultra Very Light	187
7	✣	DMC BLANK	White	818
8	▪	DMC 310	Black	27

Use 2 strands of thread for cross stitch

©2022 Maggie Smith

Reindeer

Design size: 50 x 67 stitches

N	Symbol	Number	Name	Stitches
1	◺	DMC 223	Shell Pink - Light	75
2	■	DMC 310	Black	68
3	∘	DMC 437	Tan - Light	202
4	●	DMC 680	Old Gold - Dark	39
5	□	DMC 898	Coffee Brown - Very Dark	284
6	∠	DMC 972	Canary - Deep	86
7	♡	DMC 3772	Desert Sand - Very Dark	243
8	♣	DMC 3778	Terra Cotta - Light	90
9	m	DMC 3856	Mahogany - Ultra Very Light	931
10	▽	DMC BLANK	White	4
11	=	DMC 150	Red - Bright	70

Use 2 strands of thread for cross stitch

©2022 Maggie Smith

Gingerbread Man

Design size: 46 x 69 stitches

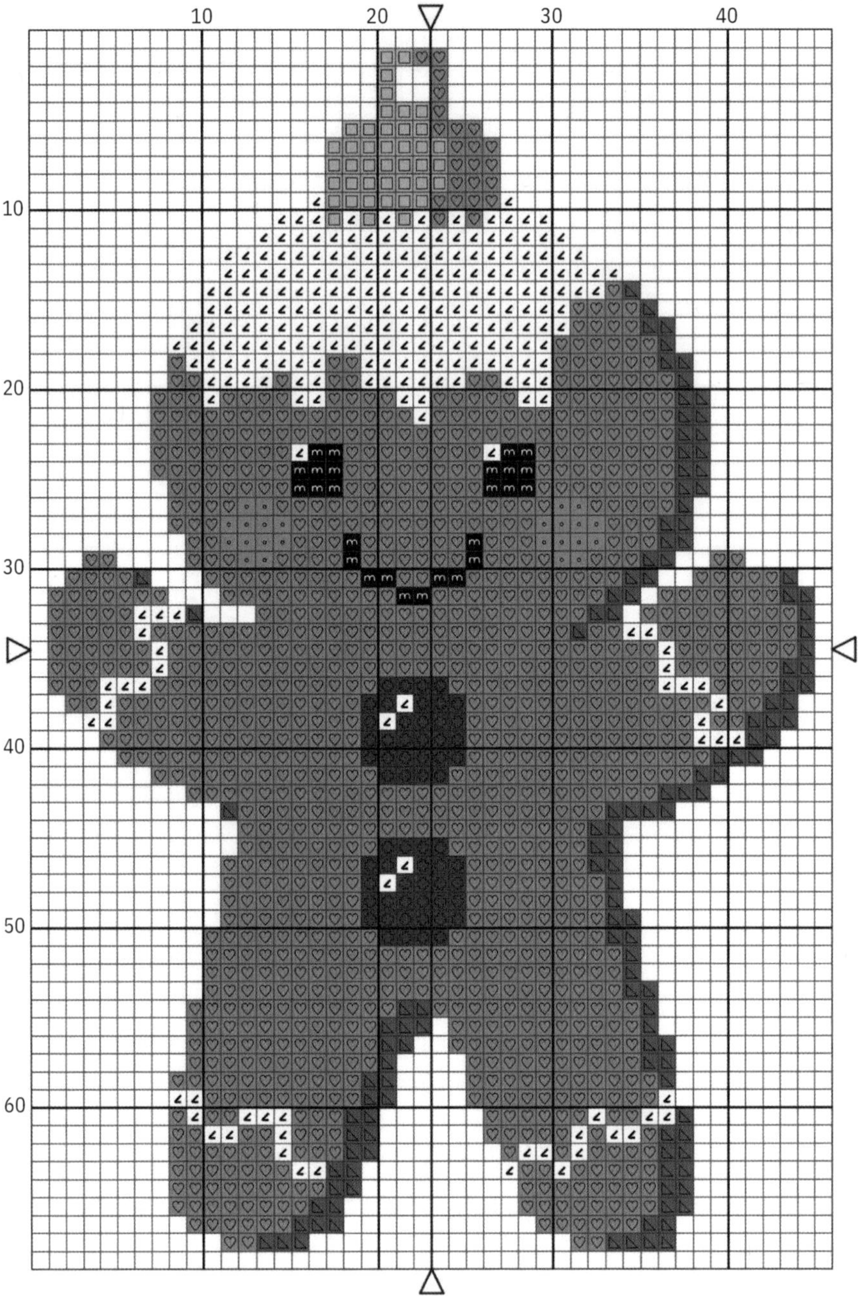

N	Symbol	Number	Name	Stitches
1	□	DMC 972	Canary - Deep	42
2	∠	DMC B5200	Snow White	259
3	m	DMC 310	Black	26
4	◺	DMC 434	Brown - Light	136
5	♡	DMC 436	Tan	1167
6	✚	DMC 817	Coral Red - Very Dark	60
7	∘	DMC 961	Dusty Rose - Dark	24

Use 2 strands of thread for cross stitch

©2022 Maggie Smith

Gingerbread Man with Suspenders

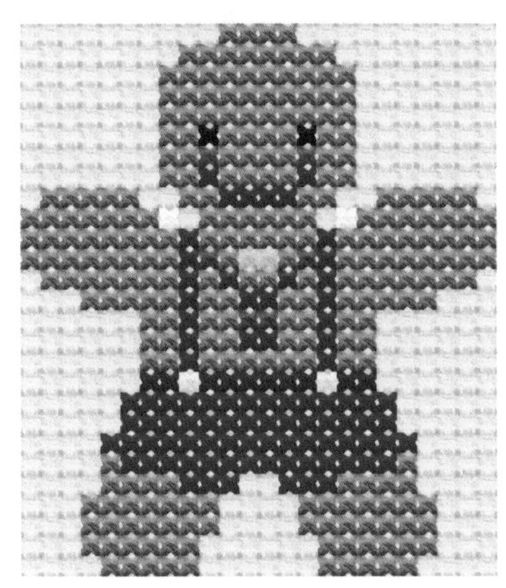

Design size: 24 x 27 stitches

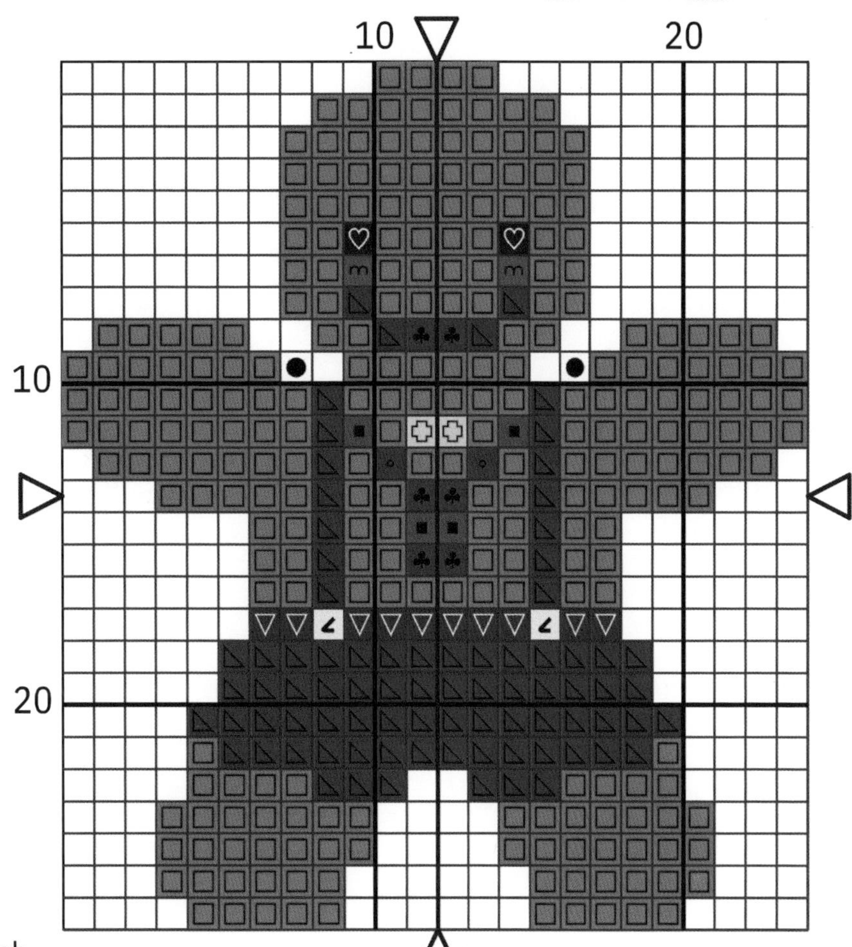

Use 2 strands of thread for cross stitch

N	Symbol		Number	Name	Stitches
1	□	□	DMC 976	Golden Brown - Medium	258
2	●	●	DMC B5200	Snow White	2
3	✚	✚	DMC 16	Chartreuse Floss - Light	2
4	▽	▽	DMC 304	Red - Medium	10
5	♣	♣	DMC 321	Red	6
6	∘	∘	DMC 347	Salmon - Very Dark	2
7	■	■	DMC 720	Orange Spice - Dark	4
8	∠	∠	DMC 746	Off White	2
9	◺	◺	DMC 817	Coral Red - Very Dark	82
10	m	m	DMC 921	Copper	2
11	♡	♡	DMC 938	Coffee Brown - Ultra Dark	2

©2022 Maggie Smith

Frosty

Design size: 50 x 65 stitches

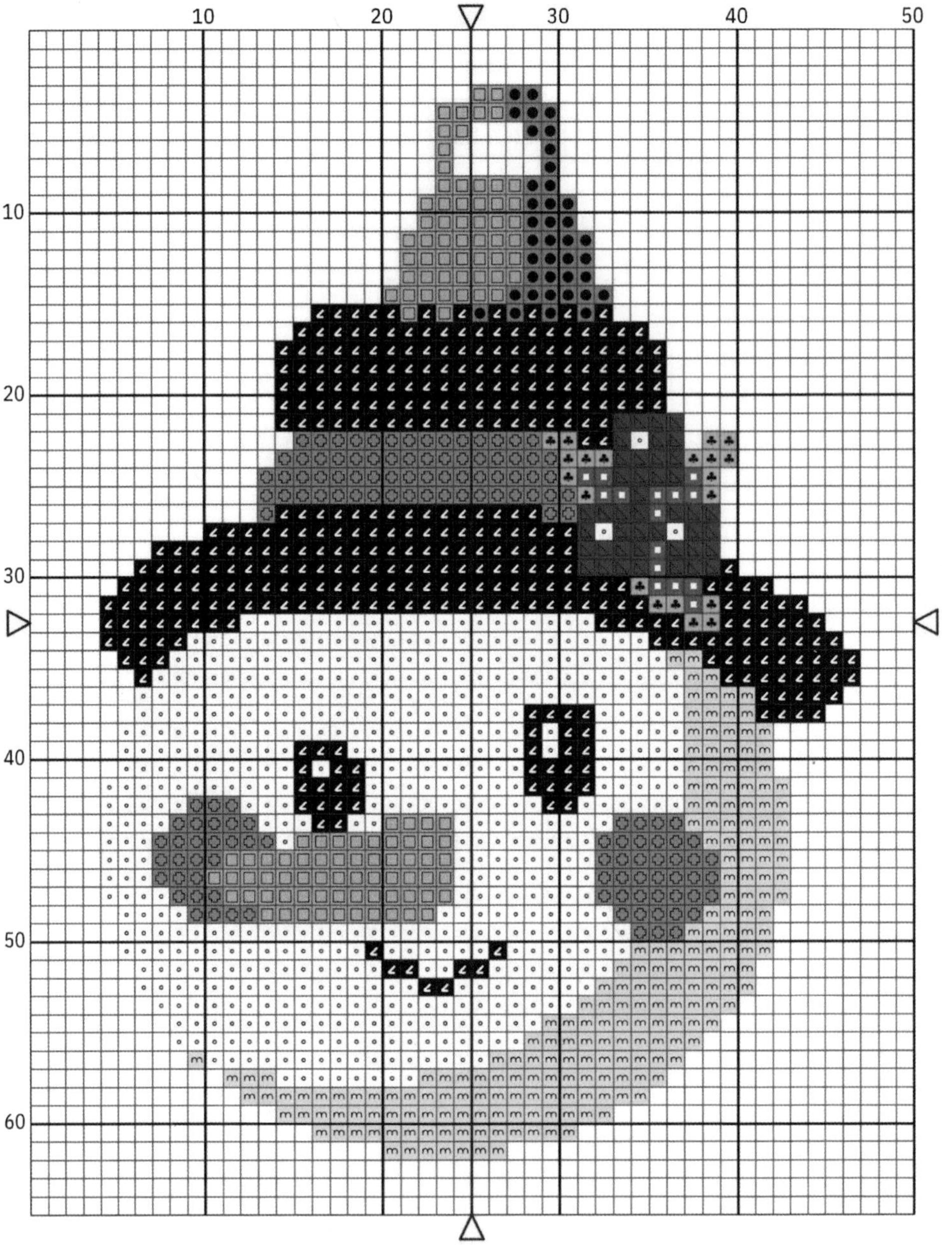

N	Symbol	Number	Name	Stitches
1	∠	DMC 310	Black	404
2	◺	DMC 321	Red	43
3	●	DMC 680	Old Gold - Dark	39
4	m	DMC 818	Baby Pink	218
5	♣	DMC 906	Parrot Green - Medium	20
6	□	DMC 972	Canary - Deep	120
7	∘	DMC B5200	Snow White	564
8	■	DMC 904	Parrot Green - Very Dark	15
9	✚	DMC 961	Dusty Rose - Dark	136

Use 2 strands of thread for cross stitch

©2022 Maggie Smith

Majestic Reindeer

Design size: 54 x 88 stitches

N	Symbol	Number	Name	Stitches
1	☐ ▣	DMC 310	BLACK	1175

Use 2 strands of thread for cross stitch

©2022 Maggie Smith

Santa Claus

Design size: 43 x 71 stitches

Use 2 strands of thread for cross stitch

N	Symbol		Number	Name	Stitches
1	▽	▽	DMC 150	Red - Bright	50
2	∘	∘	DMC 310	Black	258
3	●	●	DMC 347	Salmon - Very Dark	255
4	☆	☆	DMC 422	Hazelnut Brown - Light	11
5	♣	♣	DMC 543	Beige Brown - Ultra Very Light	119
6	7	7	DMC 725	Topaz	24
7	m	m	DMC 819	Baby Pink - Light	153
8	=	=	DMC 898	Coffee Brown - Very Dark	47
9	□	□	DMC 951	Tawny - Light	324
10	◺	◺	DMC 967	Peach - Light	130
11	╳	╳	DMC 3716	Dusty Rose - Very Light	2
12	∠	∠	DMC 3777	Terra Cotta - Very Dark	153
13	■	■	DMC 3866	Mocha Brown - Ultra Very Light	116
14	✙	✙	DMC 3882	Cocoa - Medium Light	129

©2022 Maggie Smith

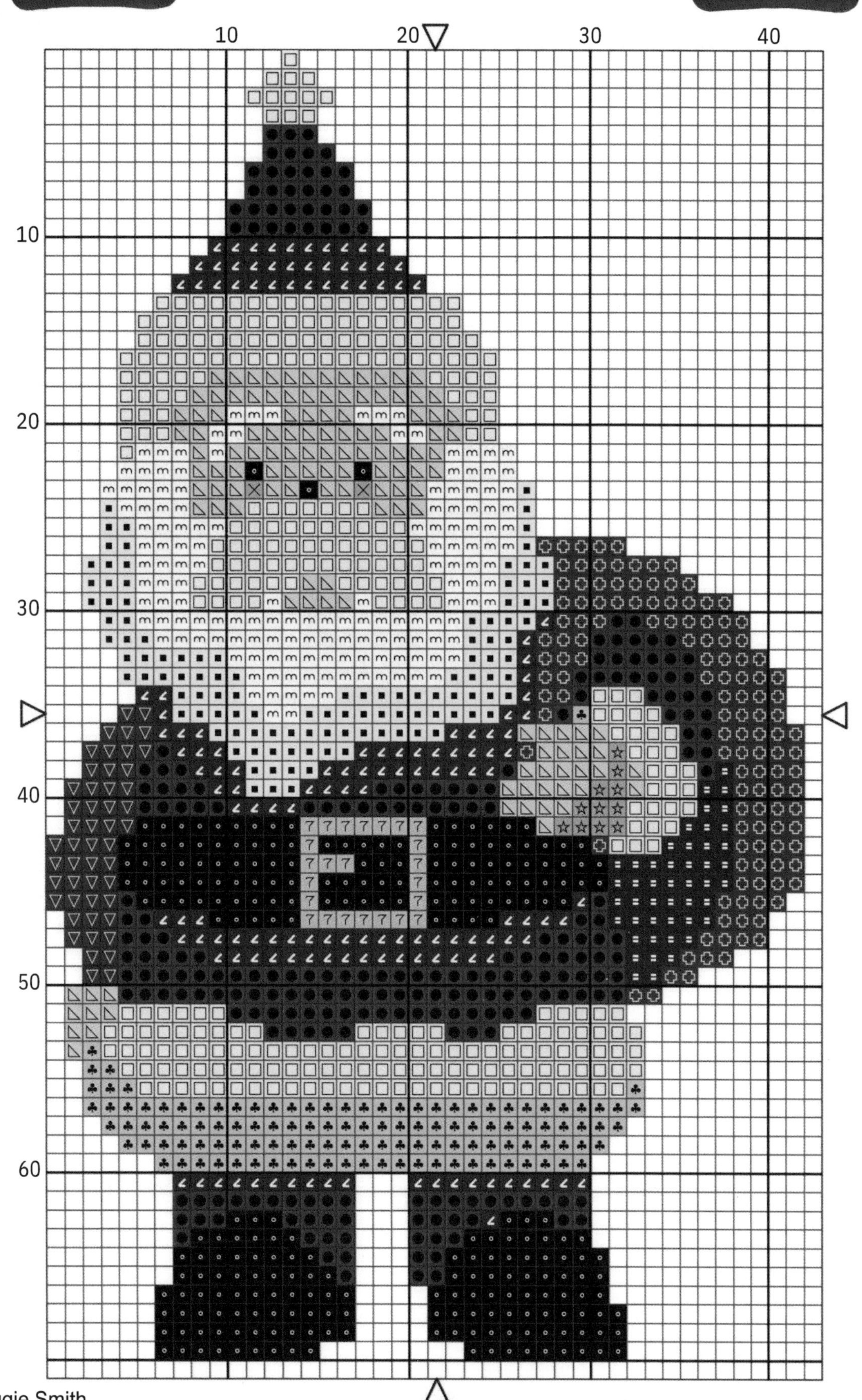

©2022 Maggie Smith

Mini Hedgehog

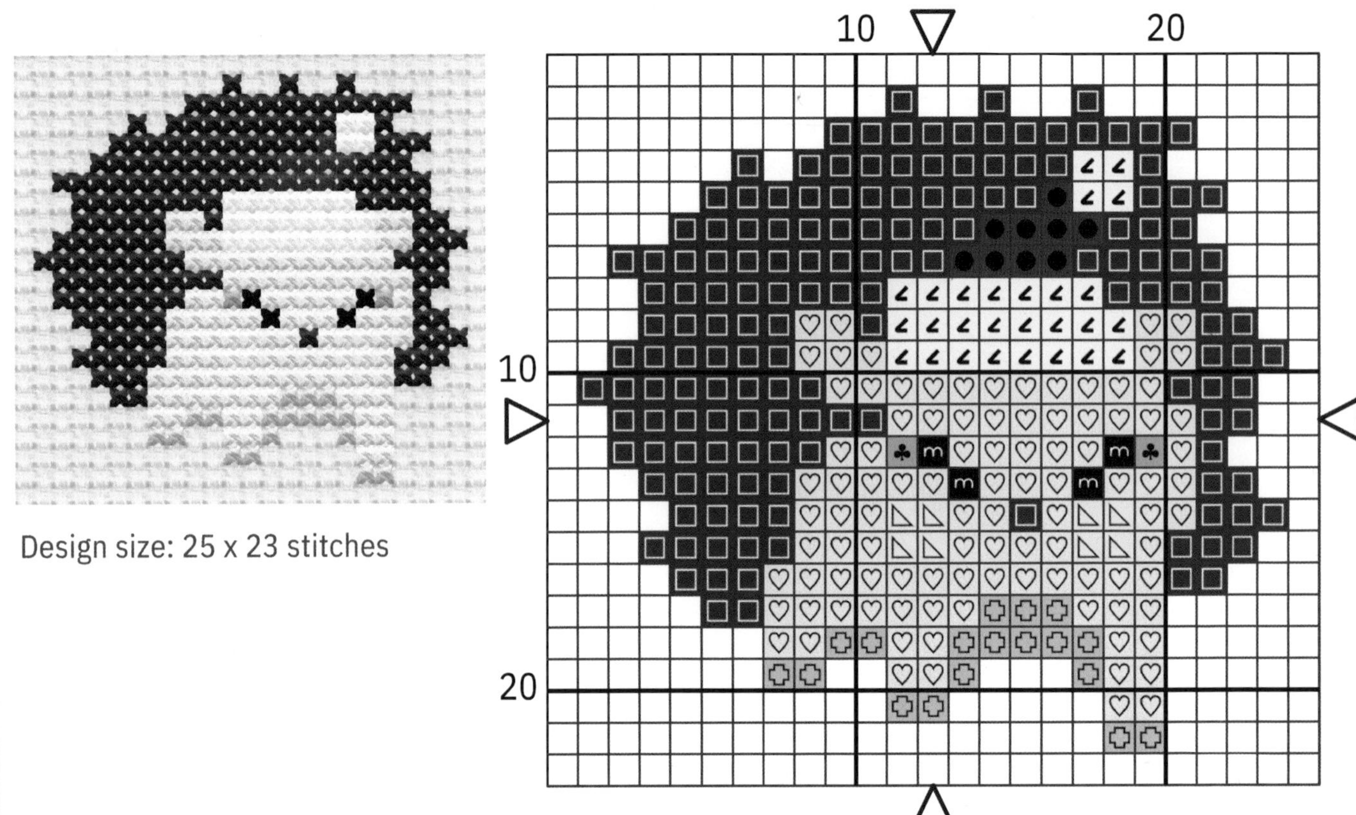

Design size: 25 x 23 stitches

Use 2 strands of thread for cross stitch

N	Symbol		Number	Name	Stitches
1	□	□	DMC 09	Cocoa - Very Dark	158
2	◺	◺	DMC 225	Shell Pink - Ultra Very Light	8
3	m	m	DMC 310	Black	4
4	●	●	DMC 347	Salmon - Very Dark	9
5	✚	✚	DMC 543	Beige Brown - Ultra Very Light	18
6	♣	♣	DMC 648	Beaver Gray - Light	2
7	♡	♡	DMC 951	Tawny - Light	100
8	∠	∠	DMC 3865	Winter White	27

©2022 Maggie Smith

Nutcracker 1

Design size: 23 x 60 stitches

Use 2 strands of thread for cross stitch

N	Symbol	Number	Name	Stitches
1	■	DMC 09	Cocoa - Very Dark	52
2	☆	DMC 21	Alizarin - Light	47
3	◊	DMC 310	Black	12
4	∠	DMC 347	Salmon - Very Dark	228
5	┏	DMC 740	Tangerine	11
6	m	DMC 754	Peach - Light	5
7	=	DMC 777	Red - Deep	14
8	✳	DMC 801	Coffee Brown - Dark	24
9	♡	DMC 816	Garnet	8
10	♣	DMC 938	Coffee Brown - Ultra Dark	124
11	✕	DMC 951	Tawny - Light	25
12	◺	DMC 967	Peach - Light	73
13	□	DMC 972	Canary - Deep	101
14	✚	DMC 976	Golden Brown - Medium	7
15	∘	DMC 3371	Black Brown	19
16	●	DMC 3852	Straw - Very Dark	19

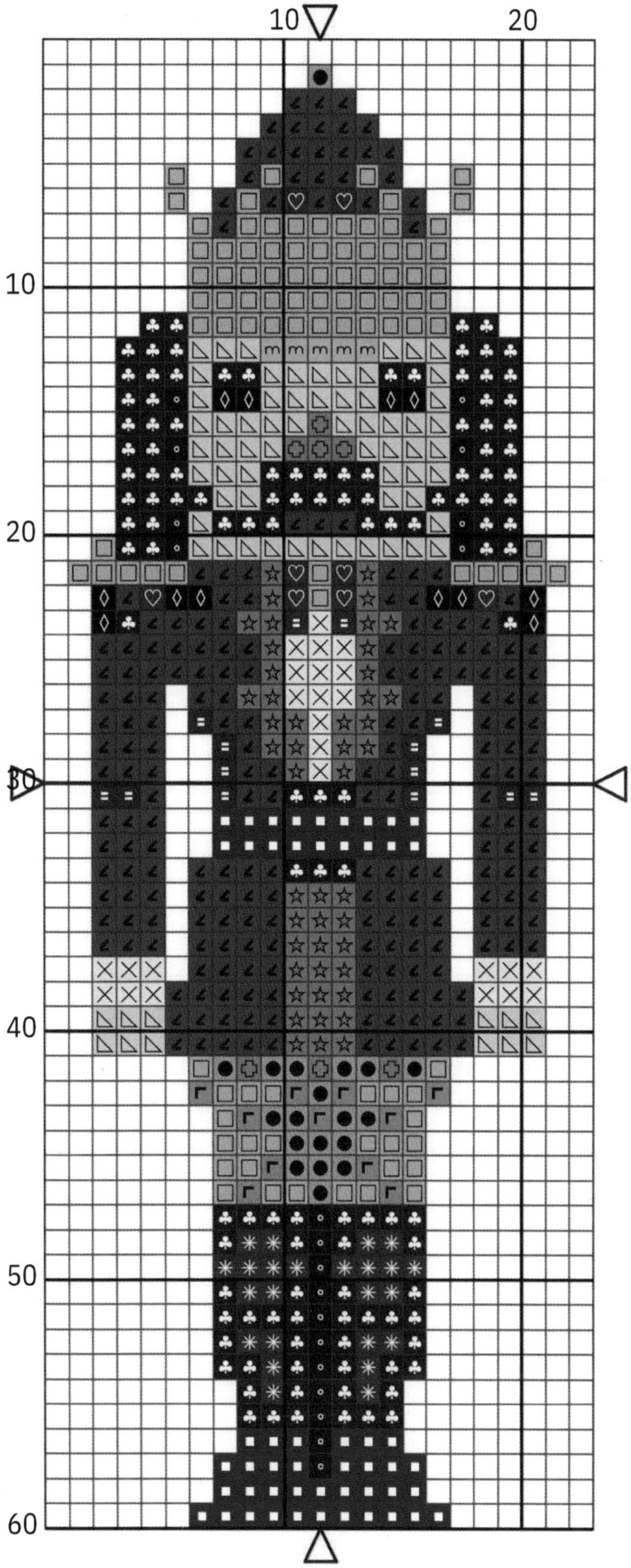

©2022 Maggie Smith

Nutcracker 2

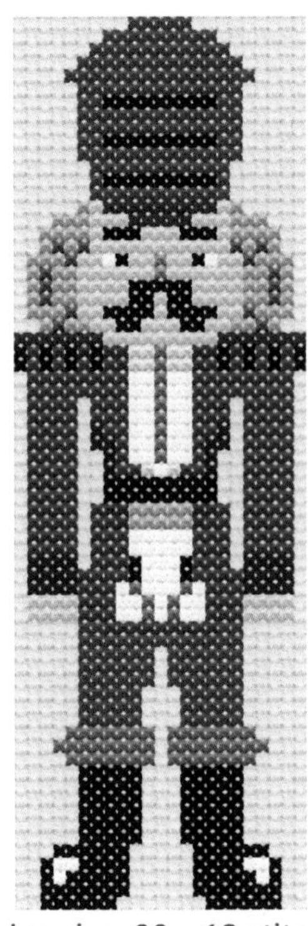

Design size: 23 x 68 stitches

Use 2 strands of thread for cross stitch

N	Symbol		Number	Name	Stitches
1	♡	♡	DMC 03	Tin - Medium	66
2	▽	▽	DMC 04	Tin - Dark	59
3	●	●	DMC 310	Black	214
4	□	□	DMC 347	Salmon - Very Dark	220
5	✚	✚	DMC 535	Ash Gray - Very Light	16
6	♣	♣	DMC 777	Red - Deep	28
7	∠	∠	DMC 919	Red Copper	9
8	◺	◺	DMC 967	Peach - Light	98
9	■	■	DMC 976	Golden Brown	2
10	☆	☆	DMC B5200	Snow White	68
11	◊	◊	DMC 158	Blue - Dark	214
12	7	7	DMC 168	Silver Gray	10
13	╳	╳	DMC 336	Blue	14
14	┏	┏	DMC 823	Blue - Dark	34

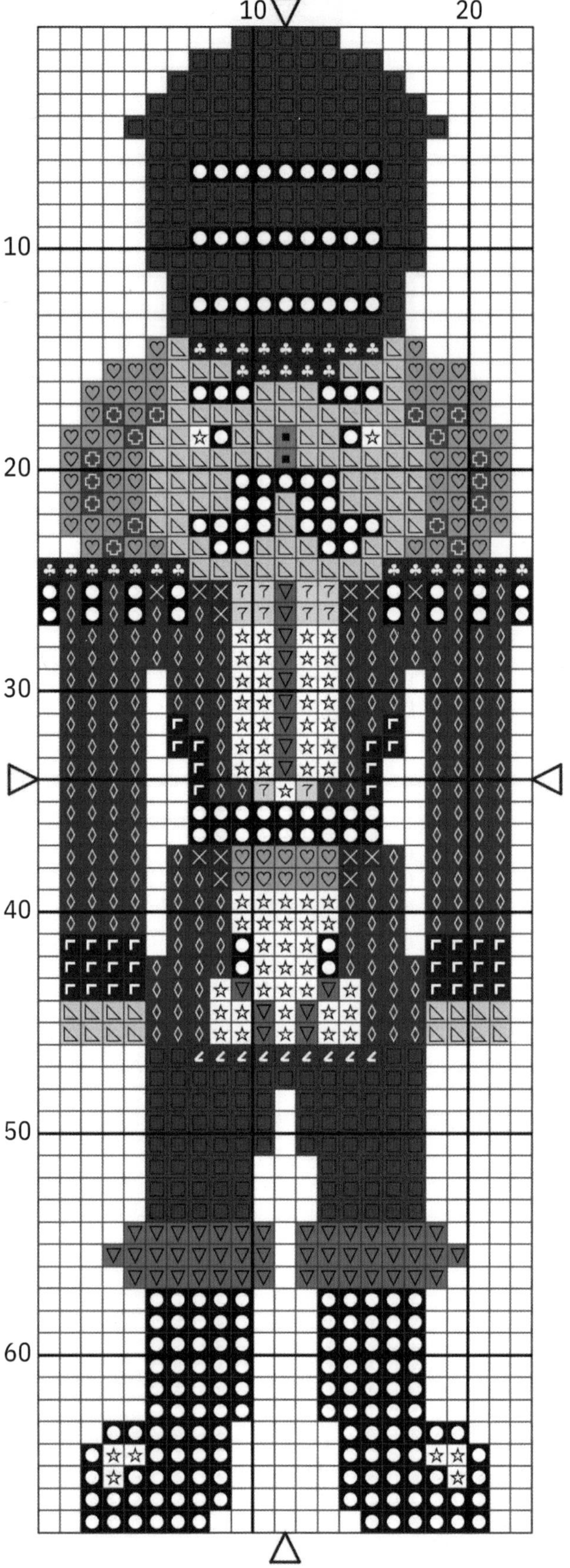

©2022 Maggie Smith

Racoon 1

Design size: 49 x 52 stitches

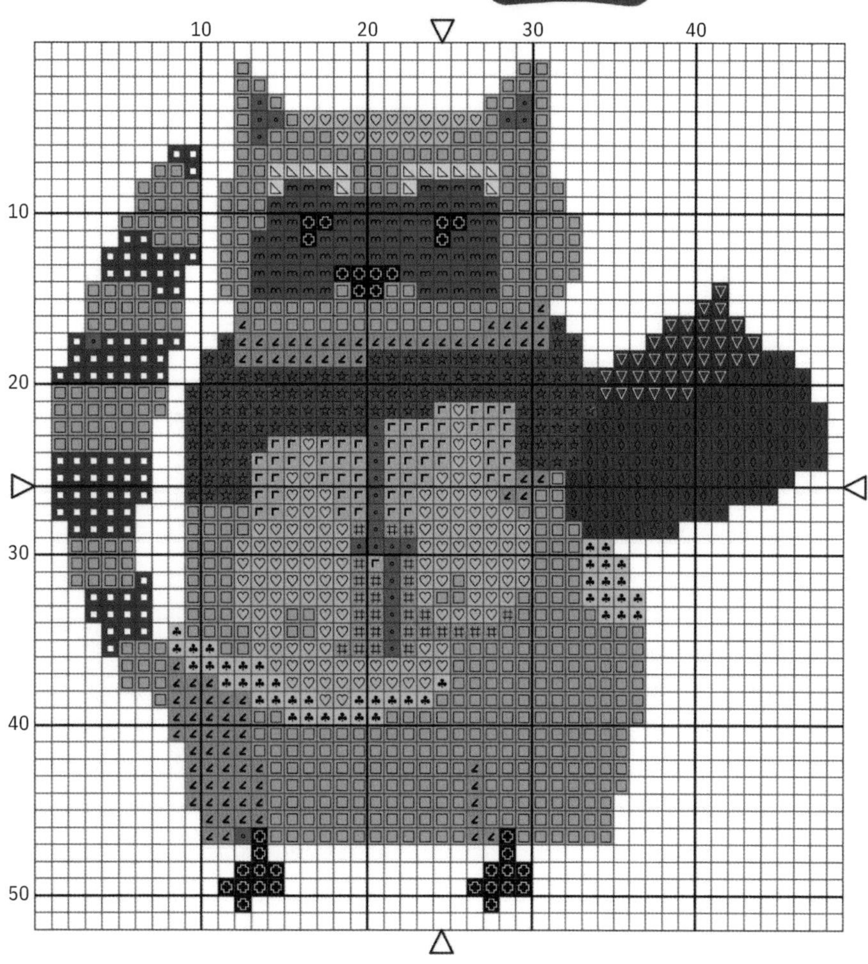

N	Symbol	Number	Name	Stitches
1	♣	DMC 01	Tin - White	45
2	▽	DMC 150	Red - Bright	38
3	✚	DMC 310	Black	32
4	◊	DMC 347	Salmon - Very Dark	116
5	m	DMC 413	Pewter Gray - Dark	80
6	♡	DMC 524	Fern Green - Very Light	155
7	□	DMC 648	Beaver Gray - Light	509
8	■	DMC 844	Beaver Gray - Ultra Dark	77
9	☆	DMC 900	Burnt Orange - Dark	128
10	⌐	DMC 972	Canary - Deep	57
11	∠	DMC 3032	Mocha Brown - Medium	87
12	◺	DMC 3072	Beaver Gray - Very Light	14
13	∘	DMC 3787	Brown Gray - Dark	26
14	#	DMC 3852	Straw - Very Dark	28

Use 2 strands of thread for cross stitch

©2022 Maggie Smith

Racoon 2

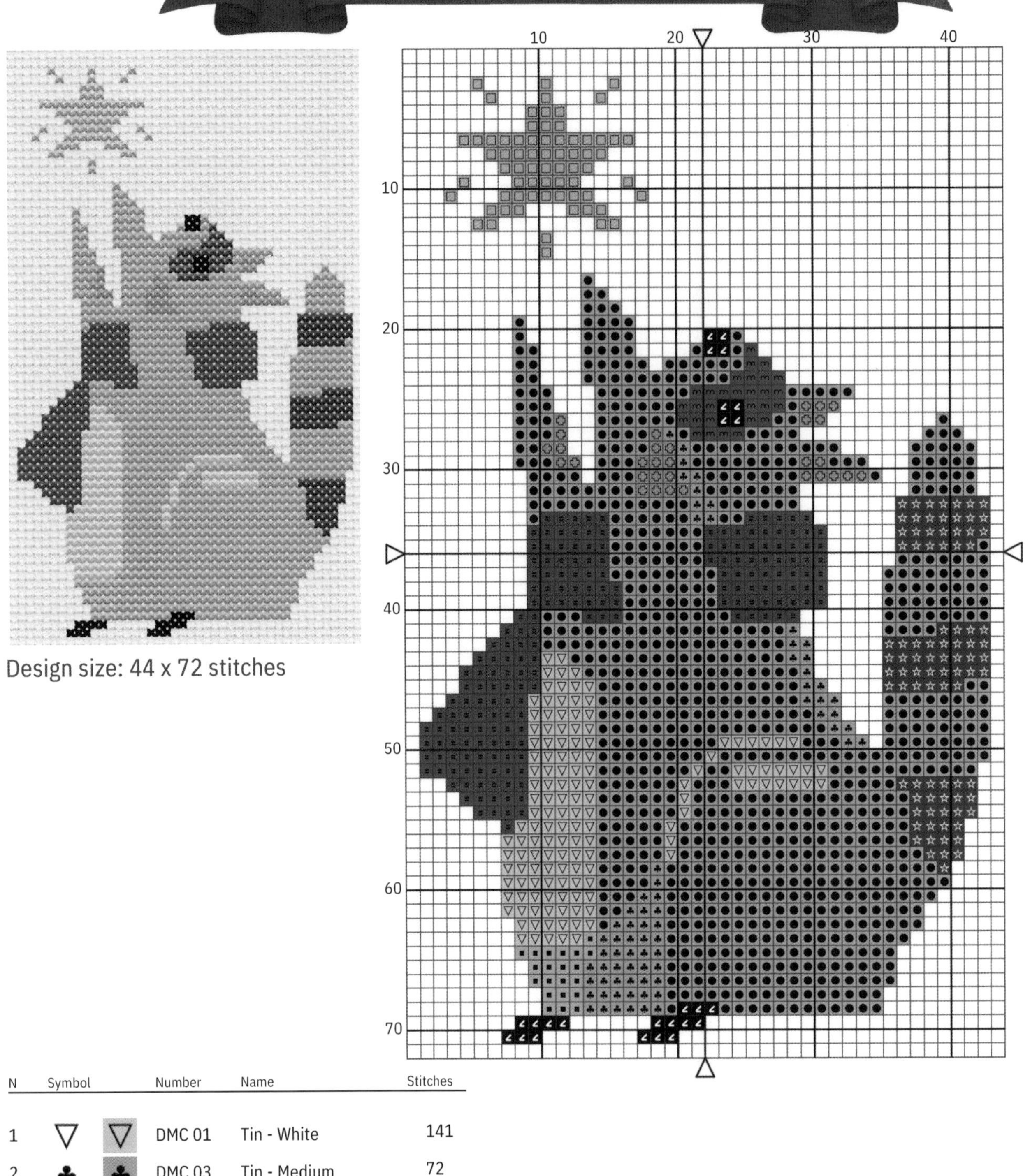

Design size: 44 x 72 stitches

N	Symbol	Number	Name	Stitches
1	▽	DMC 01	Tin - White	141
2	♣	DMC 03	Tin - Medium	72
3	∠	DMC 310	Black	25
4	m	DMC 413	Pewter Gray - Dark	29
5	■	DMC 647	Beaver Gray - Medium	21
6	●	DMC 648	Beaver Gray - Light	873
7	☆	DMC 844	Beaver Gray - Ultra Dark	89
8	=	DMC 900	Burnt Orange - Dark	194
9	□	DMC 972	Canary - Deep	69
10	✚	DMC 3032	Mocha Brown - Medium	31

Use 2 strands of thread for cross stitch

©2022 Maggie Smith

Pastel Tree

Design size: 26 x 35 stitches

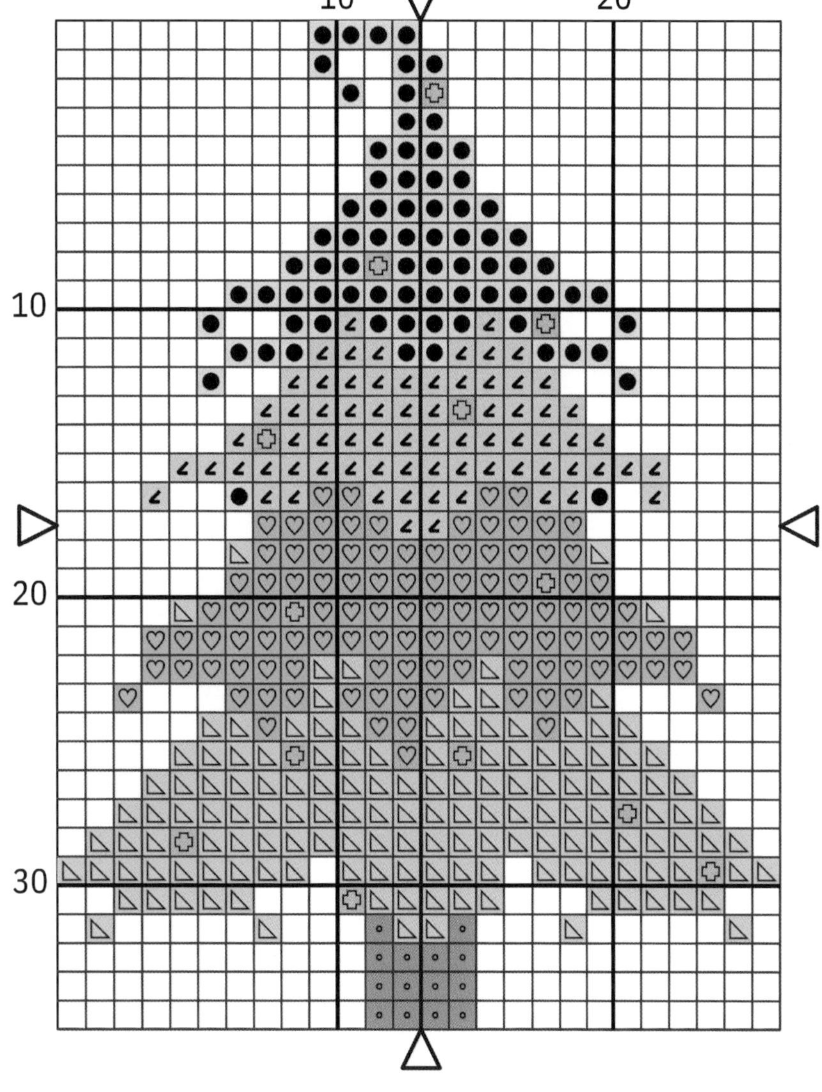

Use 2 strands of thread for cross stitch

N	Symbol		Number	Name	Stitches
1	●	●	DMC 15	Apple Green	77
2	∠	∠	DMC 164	Green - Light	72
3	✚	✚	DMC 725	Topaz	13
4	◺	◺	DMC 964	Seagreen - Light	146
5	♡	♡	DMC 993	Aquamarine - Very Light	108
6	∘	∘	DMC 3864	Mocha Beige - Light	14

©2022 Maggie Smith

Lit Tree

Design size:
27 x 40 stitches

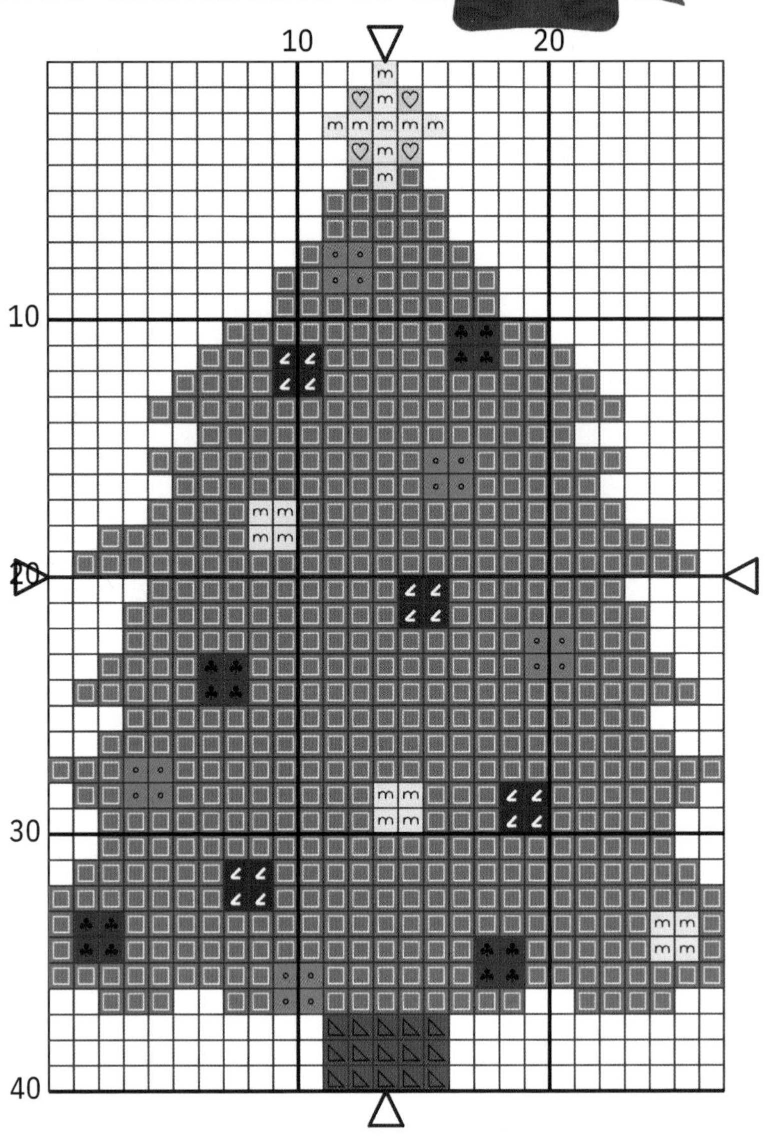

Use 2 strands of thread for cross stitch

N	Symbol	Number	Name	Stitches
1	m	DMC 307	Lemon	21
2	◺	DMC 434	Brown - Light	15
3	♡	DMC 726	Topaz - Light	4
4	♣	DMC 817	Coral Red - Very Dark	16
5	□	DMC 905	Parrot Green - Dark	558
6	∘	DMC 3844	Bright Turquoise - Dark	20
7	∠	DMC 3886	Plum - Very Dark	16

©2022 Maggie Smith

Rounded Tree

Design size: 40 x 72 stitches

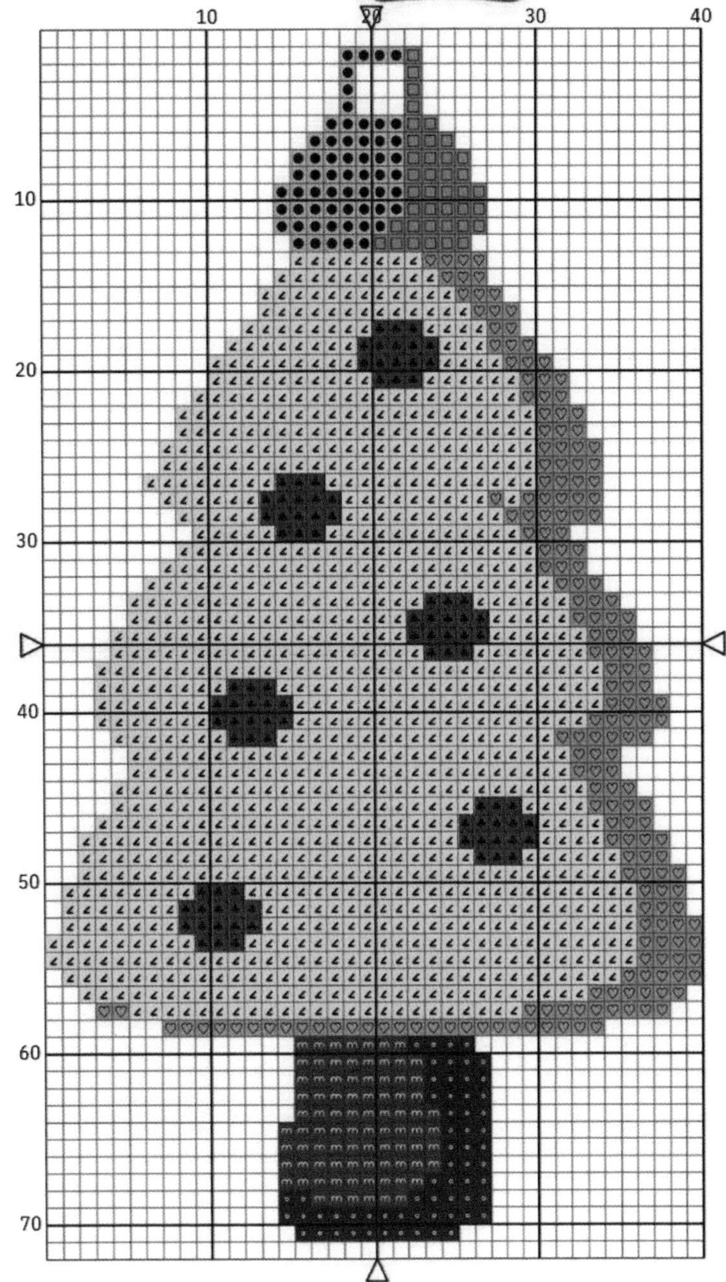

Use 2 strands of thread for cross stitch

N	Symbol	Number	Name	Stitches
1	m	DMC 400	Mahogany - Dark	85
2	♡	DMC 581	Moss Green	198
3	□	DMC 680	Old Gold - Dark	39
4	♣	DMC 817	Coral Red - Very Dark	96
5	●	DMC 972	Canary - Deep	60
6	∘	DMC 3857	Rosewood - Dark	62
7	∠	DMC 3894	Parrot Green - Very Light	1049

©2022 Maggie Smith

Holly

Design size: 88 x 40 stitches

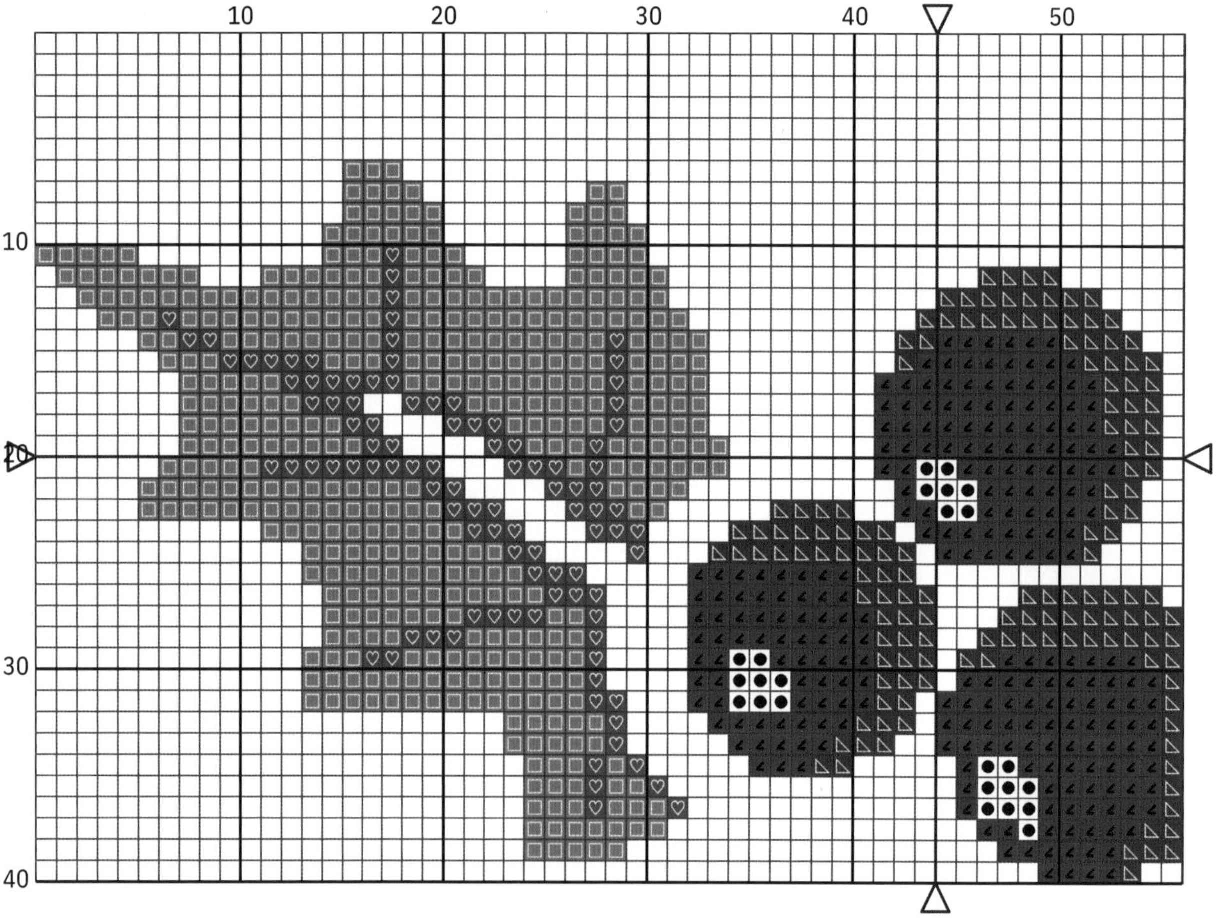

Continues on next page.

©2022 Maggie Smith

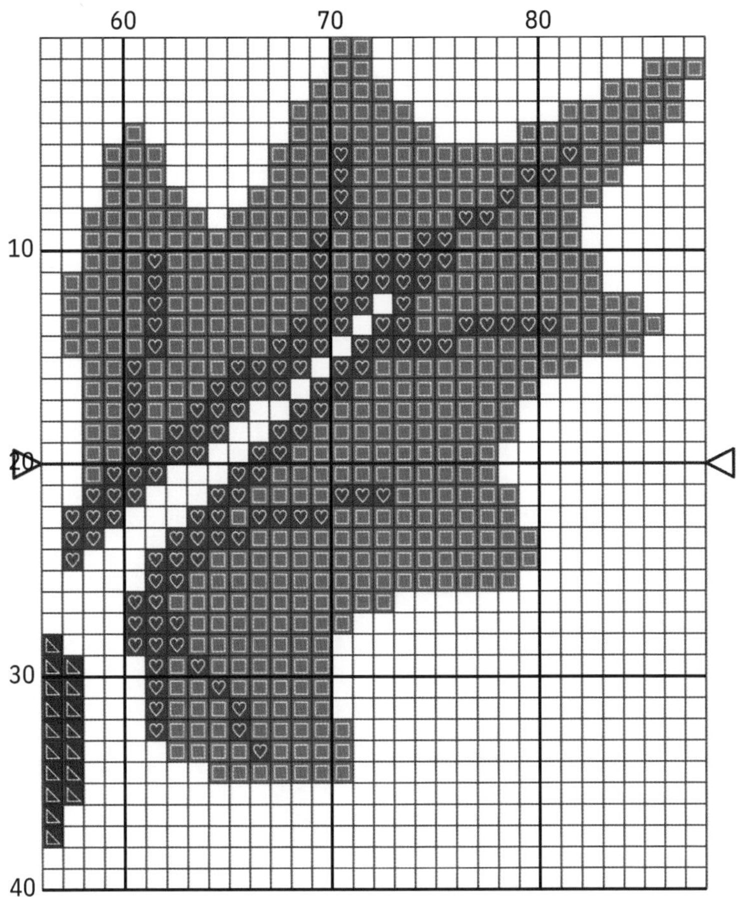

Use 2 strands of thread for cross stitch

N	Symbol		Number	Name	Stitches
1	□		DMC 905	Parrot Green - Dark	869
2	●		DMC B5200	Snow White	24
3	∠		DMC 817	Coral Red - Very Dark	256
4	◺		DMC 919	Red Copper	164
5	♡		DMC 936	Avocado Green - Very Dark	236

©2022 Maggie Smith

Wreath

10 20 30

10

20

30

40

Design size:
31 x 40 stitches

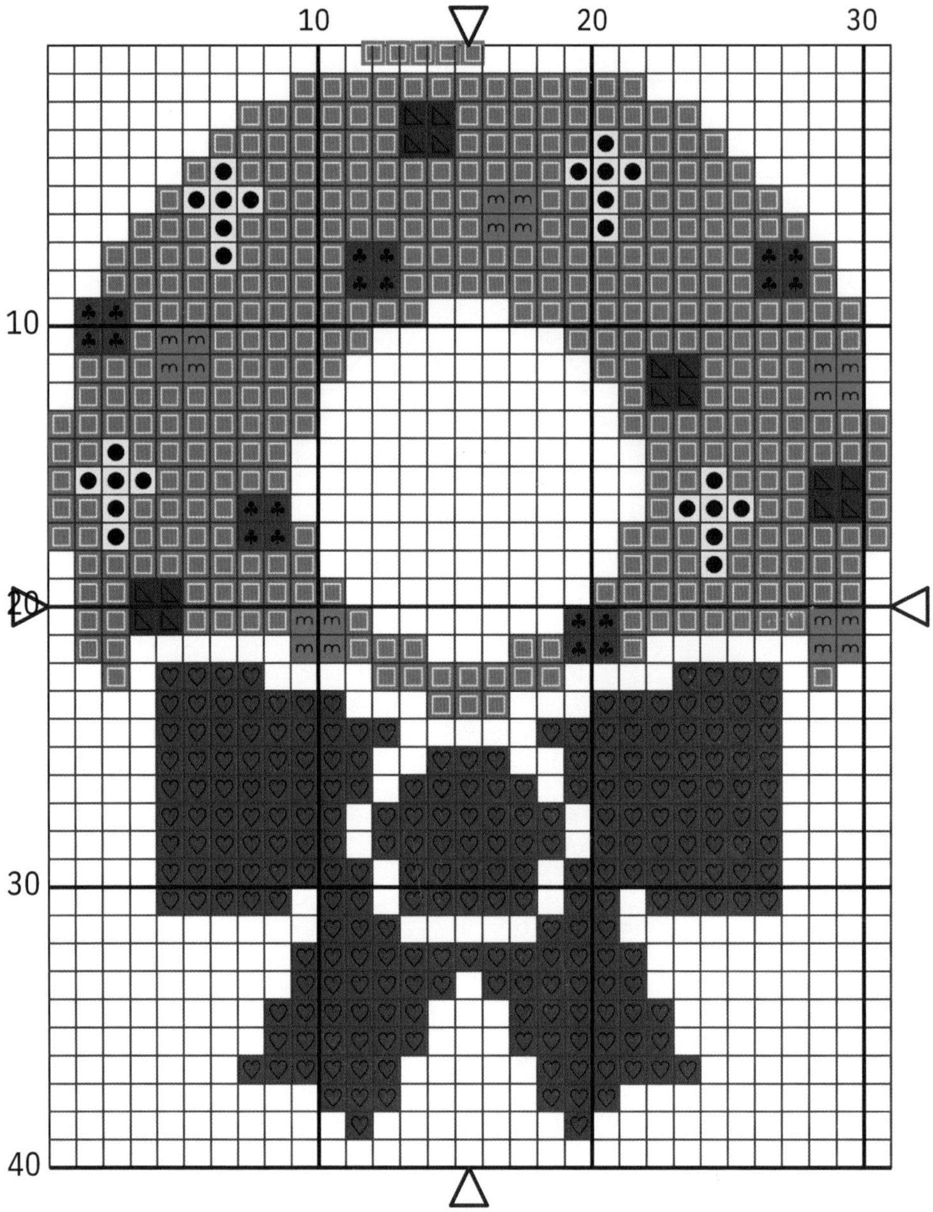

Use 2 strands of thread for cross stitch

N	Symbol	Number	Name	Stitches
1	◺	DMC 34	Fuchsia - Dark	16
2	♡	DMC 321	Red	237
3	♣	DMC 321	Red	20
4	□	DMC 905	Parrot Green - Dark	363
5	m	DMC 3843	Electric Blue	20
6	●	DMC 3889	Lemon - Medium Light	24

©2022 Maggie Smith

Bright Christmas Tree

Design size: 55 x 76 stitches

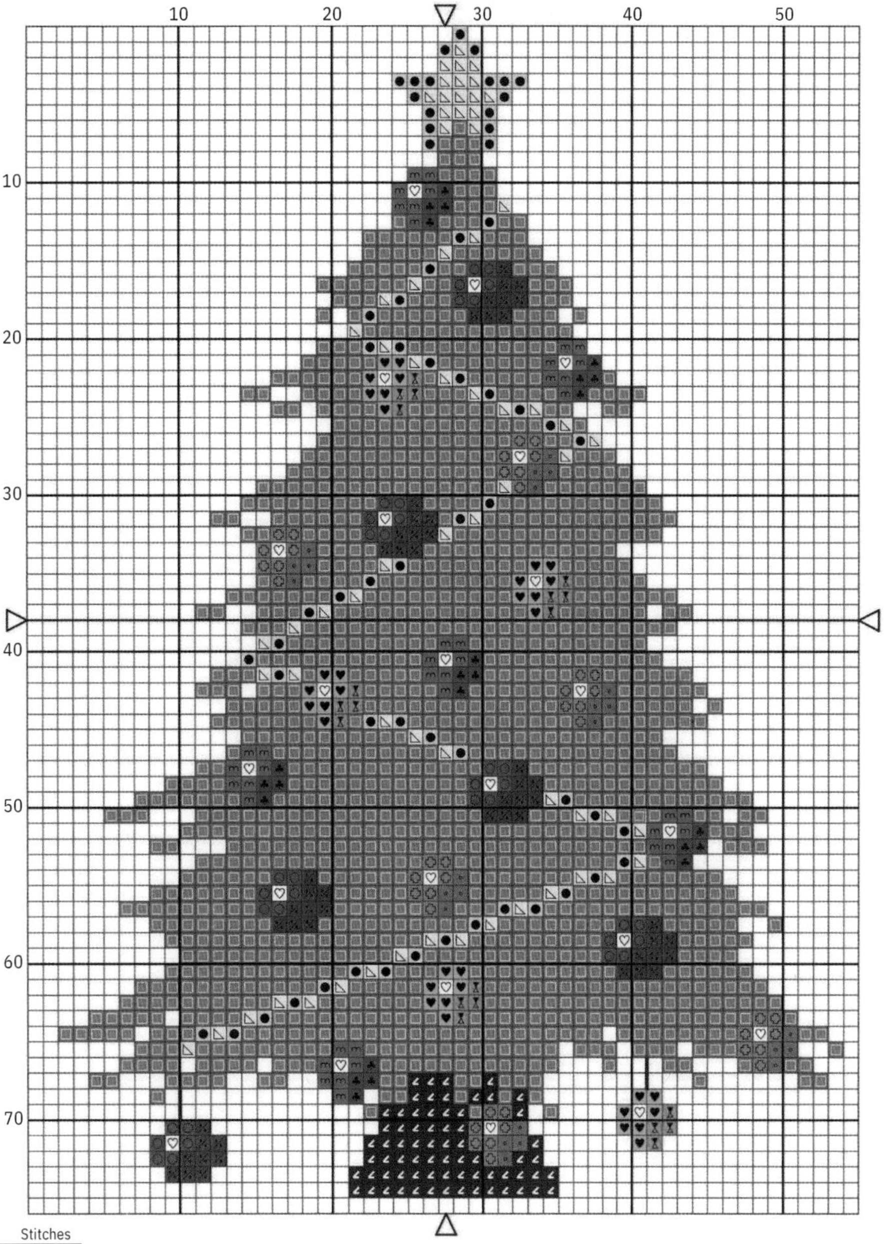

N	Symbol	Number	Name	Stitches
1	●	DMC 726	Topaz - Light	61
2	∠	DMC 898	Coffee Brown - Very Dark	69
3	□	DMC 905	Parrot Green - Dark	1313
4	♡	DMC B5200	Snow White	23
5	m	DMC 553	Violet	42
6	✚	DMC 740	Tangerine	42
7	%	DMC 817	Coral Red - Very Dark	54
8	∘	DMC 946	Burnt Orange - Medium	24
9	○	DMC 3801	Melon - Very Dark	36
10	♣	DMC 3837	Lavender - Ultra Dark	24
11	⧗	DMC 3844	Bright Turquoise - Dark	20
12	♥	DMC 3845	Bright Turquoise - Medium	35
13	◺	DMC 3889	Lemon - Medium Light	65

Use 2 strands of thread for cross stitch

©2022 Maggie Smith

All is Calm

Use 2 strands of thread for cross stitch

N	Symbol		Number	Name	Stitches
1	☐	■	DMC 310	Black	907

Design size: 64 x 72 stitches

©2022 Maggie Smith

All is Bright

Use 2 strands of thread for cross stitch

N	Symbol		Number	Name	Stitches
1	□	■	DMC 310	Black	1350

Design size: 75 x 87 stitches

10 20 30 40 50 60 70

©2022 Maggie Smith

Merry Christmas

Design size: 80 x 67 stitches

Use 2 strands of thread for cross stitch

N	Symbol		Number	Name	Stitches
1	□	■	DMC 310	Black	1444

©2022 Maggie Smith

Santa's Name

Design size: 80 x 67 stitches

Use 2 strands of thread for cross stitch

N	Symbol		Number	Name	Stitches
1	□	■	DMC 310	Black	1000

©2022 Maggie Smith

Dasher - Reindeer

Design size: 80 x 71 stitches

Use 2 strands of thread for cross stitch

N	Symbol	Number	Name	Stitches
1		DMC 310	Black	1477

©2022 Maggie Smith

Dancer - Reindeer

Design size: 80 x 74 stitches

Use 2 strands of thread for cross stitch

N	Symbol		Number	Name	Stitches
1	☐	■	DMC 310	Black	1485

Prancer - Reindeer

Design size: 80 x 67 stitches

Use 2 strands of thread for cross stitch

N	Symbol	Number	Name	Stitches
1		DMC 310	Black	1294

Vixen - Reindeer

10 20 30 40 50 60 70 80

Use 2 strands of thread for cross stitch

N	Symbol		Number	Name	Stitches
1	☐	■	DMC 310	Black	1248

Design size: 80 x 70 stitches

Comet - Reindeer

Use 2 strands of thread for cross stitch

N	Symbol		Number	Name	Stitches
1	☐	■	DMC 310	Black	1268

Design size: 80 x 68 stitches

Cupid - Reindeer

Design size: 80 x 77 stitches

Use 2 strands of thread for cross stitch

N	Symbol	Number	Name	Stitches
1	☐ ■	DMC 310	Black	1292

Donner - Reindeer

Design size: 80 x 66 stitches

Use 2 strands of thread for cross stitch

N	Symbol		Number	Name	Stitches
1	☐	■	DMC 310	Black	1346

©2022 Maggie Smith

Blitzen - Reindeer

Design size: 80 x 67 stitches

Use 2 strands of thread for cross stitch

N	Symbol		Number	Name	Stitches
1	☐	■	DMC 310	Black	1273

Rudolph - Reindeer

Design size: 80 x 71 stitches

Use 2 strands of thread for cross stitch

N	Symbol		Number	Name	Stitches
1	☐	■	DMC 310	Black	1353

Olive - The Other

Design size: 80 x 72 stitches

Use 2 strands of thread for cross stitch

N	Symbol		Number	Name	Stitches
1	☐	■	DMC 310	Black	1286

Gingerbread House Snow Globe

Design size: 40 x 47 stitches

N	Symbol		Number	Name	Stitches
1	□	□	DMC B5200	Snow White	165
2	●	●	DMC 3890	Bright Turquoise - Very Light	236
3	∠	∠	DMC BLANK	White	36
4	◺	◺	DMC 162	Baby Blue - Light	92
5	☆	☆	DMC 300	Mahogany - Very Dark	122
6	(	(	DMC 524	Fern Green - Very Light	21
7	7	7	DMC 741	Tangerine - Medium	16
8	╳	╳	DMC 742	Tangerine - Light	150
9	♡	♡	DMC 747	Sky Blue - Very Light	98
10	%	%	DMC 817	Coral Red - Very Dark	138
11	//	//	DMC 905	Parrot Green - Dark	7
12	S	S	DMC 906	Parrot Green - Medium	4
13	<	<	DMC 919	Red Copper	17
14	m	m	DMC 964	Seagreen - Light	79
15	#	#	DMC 972	Canary - Deep	24
16	▽	▽	DMC 975	Golden Brown - Dark	58
17	○	○	DMC 976	Golden Brown - Medium	184
18	♣	♣	DMC 3753	Antique Blue - Ultra Very Light	89
19	⧗	⧗	DMC 3844	Bright Turquoise - Dark	3
20	♥	♥	DMC 3845	Bright Turquoise - Medium	5

Use 2 strands of thread for cross stitch

©2022 Maggie Smith

Gingerbread House Snow Globe

Use 1 strand of thread for backstitch

N	Line style	Number	Name	Units
1		DMC B5200	Snow White	1
2		DMC 300	Mahogany - Very Dark	48
3		DMC 666	Red - Bright	67
4		DMC 817	Coral Red - Very Dark	50

©2022 Maggie Smith

Gingerbread Man Snow Globe

Design size: 40 x 47 stitches

N	Symbol		Number	Name	Stitches
1	□	□	DMC B5200	Snow White	117
2	●	●	DMC 3890	Bright Turquoise - Very Light	236
3	∠	∠	DMC BLANK	White	45
4	%	%	DMC 16	Chartreuse Floss - Light	2
5	◺	◺	DMC 162	Baby Blue - Light	135
6	☆	☆	DMC 300	Mahogany - Very Dark	107
7	//	//	DMC 304	Red - Medium	10
8	<	<	DMC 321	Red	6
9	○	○	DMC 347	Salmon - Very Dark	2
10	S	S	DMC 434	Brown - Light	24
11	(	(	DMC 720	Orange Spice - Dark	4
12	♥	♥	DMC 741	Tangerine - Medium	16
13	⧗	⧗	DMC 742	Tangerine - Light	88
14	♡	♡	DMC 747	Sky Blue - Very Light	87
15	✳	✳	DMC 817	Coral Red - Very Dark	80
16	#	#	DMC 921	Copper	2
17	⌜	⌜	DMC 938	Coffee Brown - Ultra Dark	2
18	m	m	DMC 964	Seagreen - Light	77
19	°	°	DMC 972	Canary - Deep	64
20	▽	▽	DMC 975	Golden Brown - Dark	49
21	✕	✕	DMC 976	Golden Brown - Medium	251
22	♣	♣	DMC 3753	Antique Blue - Ultra Very Light	142

Use 2 strands of thread for cross stitch

©2022 Maggie Smith

Gingerbread Man Snow Globe

©2022 Maggie Smith

Glowing Tree Snow Globe

Design size: 40 x 47 stitches

Use 2 strands of thread for cross stitch

N	Symbol		Number	Name	Stitches
1	□	□	DMC B5200	Snow White	107
2	●	●	DMC 3890	Bright Turquoise - Very Light	235
3	∠	∠	DMC BLANK	White	5
4	♥	♥	DMC 12	Tender Green	69
5	◺	◺	DMC 162	Baby Blue - Light	160
6	%	%	DMC 300	Mahogany - Very Dark	107
7	<	<	DMC 307	Lemon	142
8	×	×	DMC 434	Brown - Light	33
9	⧗	⧗	DMC 445	Lemon - Light	77
10	⌜	⌜	DMC 550	Violet - Very Dark	4
11	✳	✳	DMC 666	Red - Bright	4
12	//	//	DMC 741	Tangerine - Medium	16
13	(	(	DMC 742	Tangerine - Light	88
14	♡	♡	DMC 747	Sky Blue - Very Light	71
15	7	7	DMC 906	Parrot Green - Medium	111
16	m	m	DMC 964	Seagreen - Light	79
17	∘	∘	DMC 972	Canary - Deep	67
18	○	○	DMC 975	Golden Brown - Dark	49
19	♣	♣	DMC 3753	Antique Blue - Ultra Very Light	46
20	#	#	DMC 3843	Electric Blue	4
21	S	S	DMC 3889	Lemon - Medium Light	72

©2022 Maggie Smith

©2022 Maggie Smith

Gnome Snow Globe

Design size: 40 x 47 stitches

Use 2 strands of thread for cross stitch

N	Symbol		Number	Name	Stitches
1	□	□	DMC B5200	Snow White	108
2	◺	◺	DMC 162	Baby Blue - Light	103
3	☆	☆	DMC 300	Mahogany - Very Dark	122
4	⧗	⧗	DMC 326	Rose - Very Dark	25
5	✳	✳	DMC 701	Green - Light	72
6	7	7	DMC 741	Tangerine - Medium	16
7	×	×	DMC 742	Tangerine - Light	149
8	(	(	DMC 762	Pearl Gray - Very Light	35
9	♥	♥	DMC 777	Red - Deep	18
10	S	S	DMC 816	Garnet	37
11	#	#	DMC 817	Coral Red - Very Dark	21
12	m	m	DMC 964	Seagreen - Light	77
13	%	%	DMC 967	Peach - Light	4
14	▽	▽	DMC 975	Golden Brown - Dark	58
15	//	//	DMC 3024	Brown Gray - Very Light	57
16	↑	↑	DMC 3371	Black Brown	33
17	♣	♣	DMC 3753	Antique Blue - Ultra Very Light	144
18	┏	┏	DMC 3818	Emerald Green - Ultra Very Dark	64
19	■	■	DMC 3821	Straw	1
20	○	○	DMC 3824	Apricot - Light	12
21	>	>	DMC 3854	Autumn Gold - Medium	11
22	●	●	DMC 3890	Bright Turquoise - Very Light	237
23	∠	∠	DMC BLANK	White	53
24	♡	♡	DMC 747	Sky Blue - Very Light	89

©2022 Maggie Smith

Gnome Snow Globe

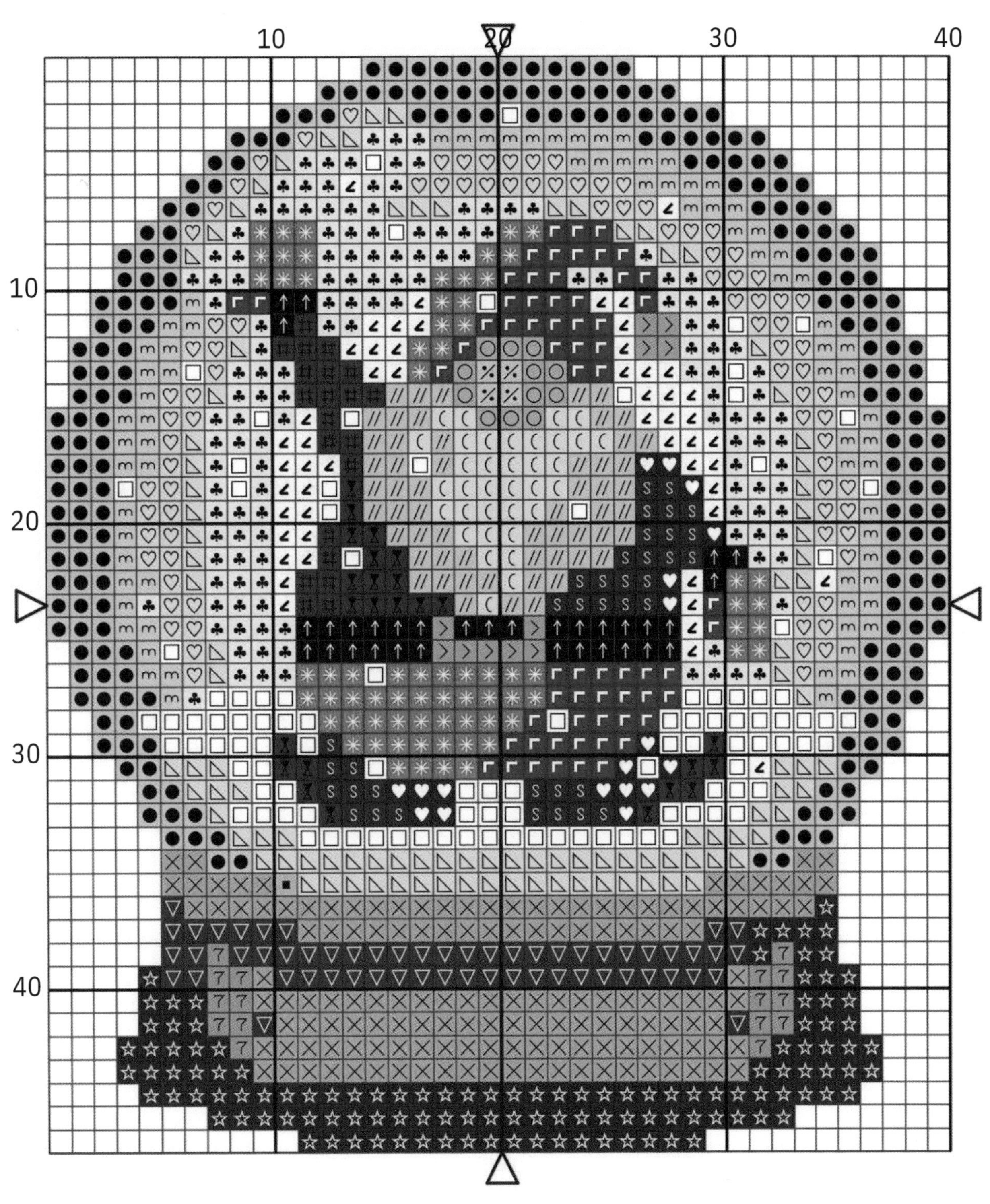

©2022 Maggie Smith

Design size: 40 x 47 stitches

Use 2 strands of thread for cross stitch

N	Symbol		Number	Name	Stitches
1	□	□	DMC B5200	Snow White	116
2	●	●	DMC 3890	Bright Turquoise - Very Light	236
3	∠	∠	DMC BLANK	White	5
4	◺	◺	DMC 162	Baby Blue - Light	134
5	☆	☆	DMC 300	Mahogany - Very Dark	136
6	♥	♥	DMC 550	Violet - Very Dark	8
7	(	(	DMC 644	Beige Gray - Medium	24
8	7	7	DMC 741	Tangerine - Medium	38
9	✕	✕	DMC 742	Tangerine - Light	161
10	♡	♡	DMC 747	Sky Blue - Very Light	84
11	<	<	DMC 817	Coral Red - Very Dark	84
12	S	S	DMC 820	Royal Blue - Very Dark	8
13	✳	✳	DMC 840	Beige Brown - Medium	32
14	%	%	DMC 904	Parrot Green - Very Dark	65
15	┏	┏	DMC 919	Red Copper	61
16	m	m	DMC 964	Seagreen - Light	76
17	▽	▽	DMC 975	Golden Brown - Dark	58
18	⧗	⧗	DMC 3023	Brown Gray - Light	14
19	♣	♣	DMC 3753	Antique Blue - Ultra Very Light	206

©2022 Maggie Smith

House Snow Globe

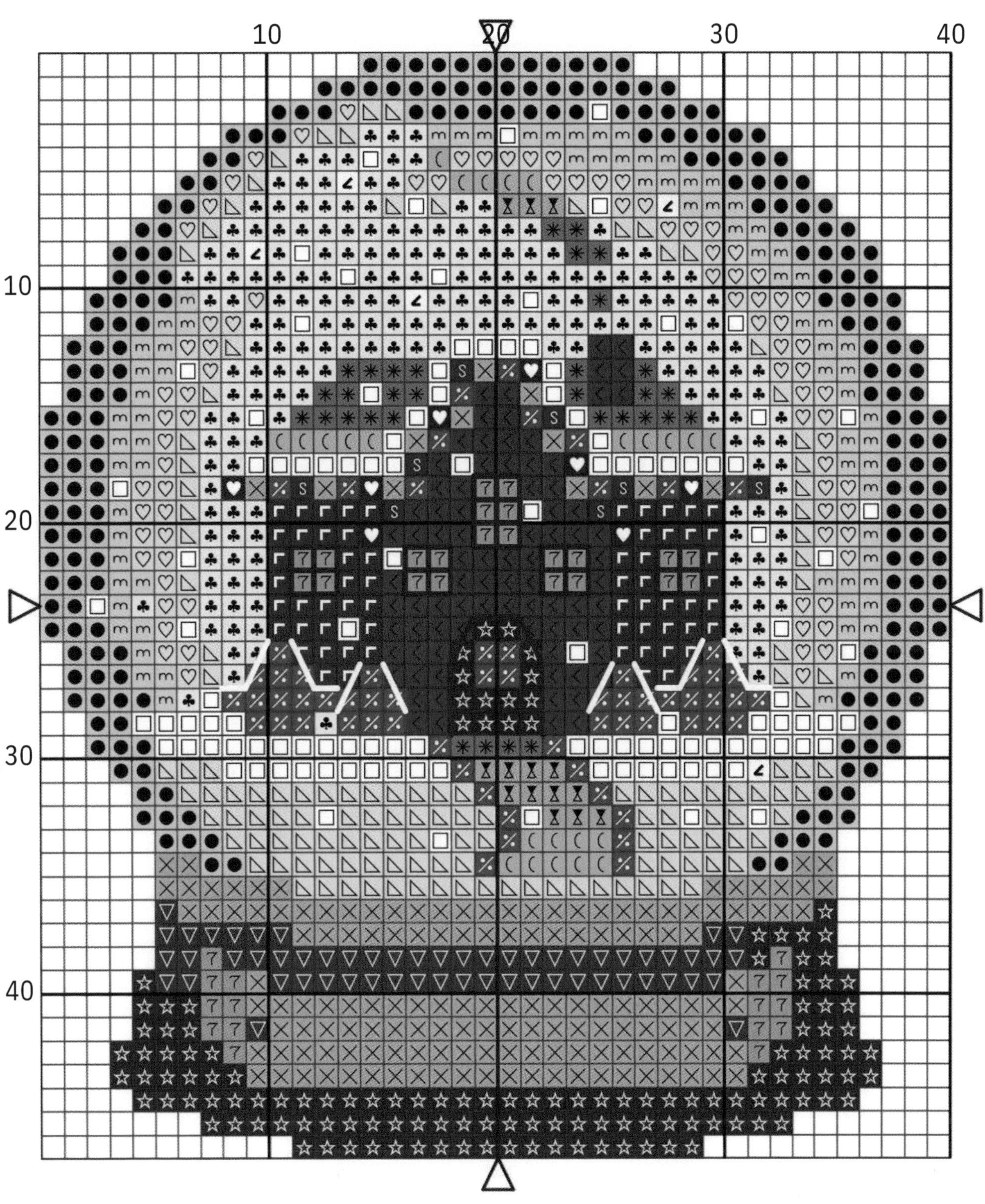

©2022 Maggie Smith

Penguin Snow Globe

Design size: 40 x 47 stitches

Use 2 strands of thread for cross stitch

N	Symbol		Number	Name	Stitches
1	□	□	DMC B5200	Snow White	251
2	●	●	DMC 3890	Bright Turquoise - Very Light	234
3	∠	∠	DMC BLANK	White	3
4	◺	◺	DMC 162	Baby Blue - Light	100
5	☆	☆	DMC 300	Mahogany - Very Dark	122
6	┌	┌	DMC 310	Black	70
7	✳	✳	DMC 321	Red	59
8	7	7	DMC 741	Tangerine - Medium	16
9	╳	╳	DMC 742	Tangerine - Light	150
10	♡	♡	DMC 747	Sky Blue - Very Light	94
11	m	m	DMC 964	Seagreen - Light	83
12	#	#	DMC 972	Canary - Deep	19
13	▽	▽	DMC 975	Golden Brown - Dark	58
14	<	<	DMC 3024	Brown Gray - Very Light	34
15	♣	♣	DMC 3753	Antique Blue - Ultra Very Light	253

©2022 Maggie Smith

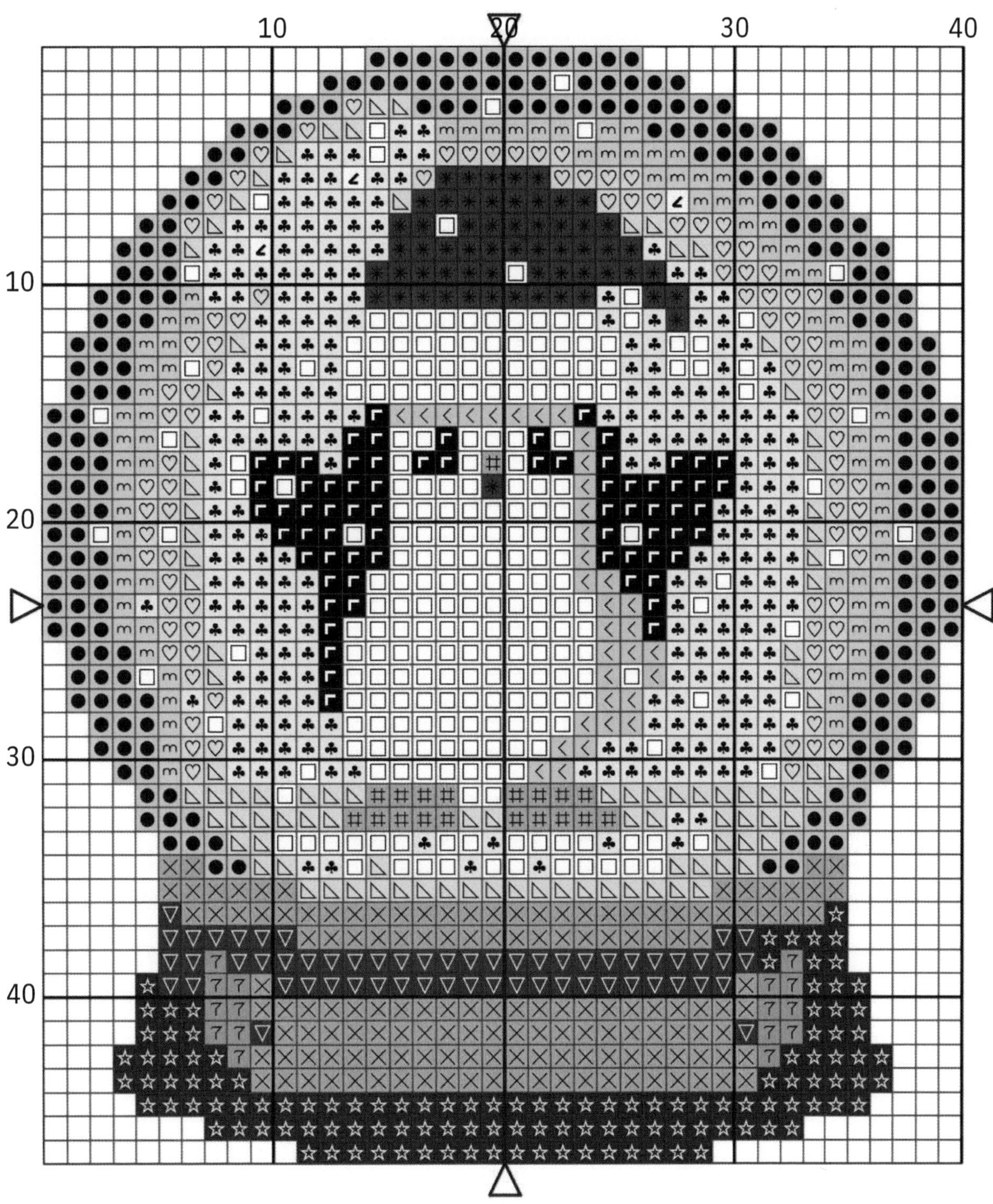

©2022 Maggie Smith

Reindeer Snow Globe

Design size: 40 x 47 stitches

Use 2 strands of thread for cross stitch

N	Symbol		Number	Name	Stitches
1	□	□	DMC B5200	Snow White	58
2	◺	◺	DMC 162	Baby Blue - Light	117
3	☆	☆	DMC 300	Mahogany - Very Dark	122
4	✳	✳	DMC 301	Mahogany - Medium	38
5	S	S	DMC 310	Black	6
6	♥	♥	DMC 321	Red	2
7	//	//	DMC 648	Beaver Gray - Light	2
8	T	T	DMC 741	Tangerine - Medium	16
9	✚	✚	DMC 742	Tangerine - Light	149
10	7	7	DMC 905	Parrot Green - Dark	84
11	┏	┏	DMC 907	Parrot Green - Light	79
12	<	<	DMC 922	Copper - Light	94
13	✕	✕	DMC 936	Avocado Green - Very Dark	73
14	○	○	DMC 950	Desert Sand - Light	16
15	m	m	DMC 964	Seagreen - Light	78
16	▽	▽	DMC 975	Golden Brown - Dark	58
17	↑	↑	DMC 3712	Salmon - Medium	2
18	♣	♣	DMC 3753	Antique Blue - Ultra Very Light	122
19	>	>	DMC 3776	Mahogany - Light	8
20	■	■	DMC 3821	Straw	1
21	#	#	DMC 3825	Pumpkin - Pale	8
22	⧗	⧗	DMC 3858	Rosewood - Medium	5
23	(	(	DMC 3866	Mocha Brown - Ultra Very Light	34
24	⁒	⁒	DMC 3883	Copper - Medium Light	38
25	●	●	DMC 3890	Bright Turquoise - Very Light	238
26	∠	∠	DMC BLANK	White	16
27	♡	♡	DMC 747	Sky Blue - Very Light	82

©2022 Maggie Smith

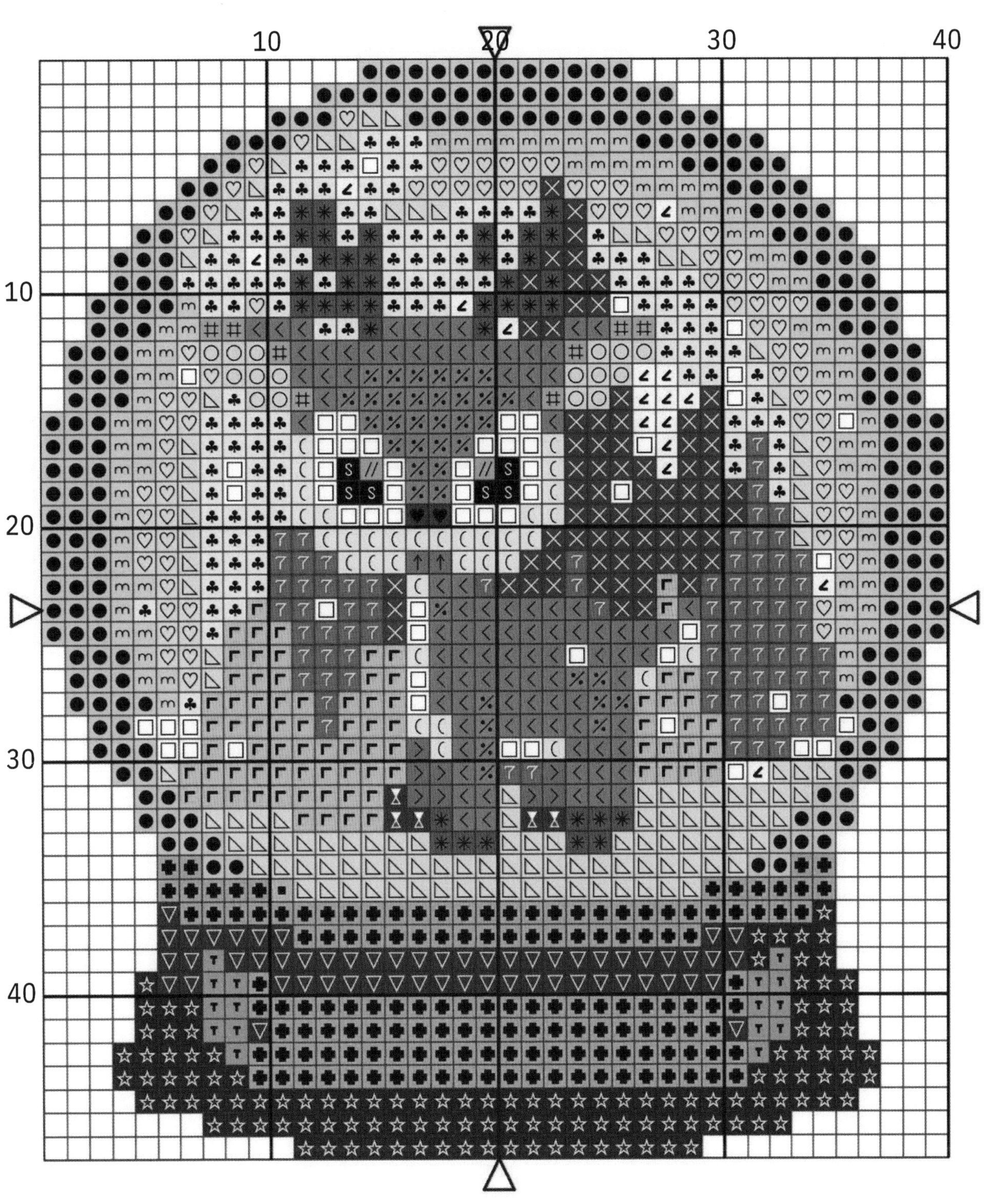

©2022 Maggie Smith

Tree and Presents Snow Globe

Design size: 40 x 47 stitches

Use 2 strands of thread for cross stitch

N	Symbol		Number	Name	Stitches
1	□	□	DMC B5200	Snow White	55
2	●	●	DMC 3890	Bright Turquoise - Very Light	234
3	∠	∠	DMC BLANK	White	6
4	◺	◺	DMC 162	Baby Blue - Light	76
5	☆	☆	DMC 300	Mahogany - Very Dark	127
6	<	<	DMC 321	Red	18
7	S	S	DMC 550	Violet - Very Dark	10
8	//	//	DMC 552	Violet - Medium	12
9	○	○	DMC 666	Red - Bright	4
10	✳	✳	DMC 726	Topaz - Light	31
11	7	7	DMC 741	Tangerine - Medium	48
12	╳	╳	DMC 742	Tangerine - Light	162
13	♡	♡	DMC 747	Sky Blue - Very Light	80
14	%	%	DMC 820	Royal Blue - Very Dark	4
15	┏	┏	DMC 905	Parrot Green - Dark	162
16	#	#	DMC 936	Avocado Green - Very Dark	80
17	m	m	DMC 964	Seagreen - Light	76
18	▽	▽	DMC 975	Golden Brown - Dark	65
19	♣	♣	DMC 3753	Antique Blue - Ultra Very Light	288
20	(	(	DMC 3891	Bright Turquoise - Very Dark	8

©2022 Maggie Smith

Tree and Presents Snow Globe

©2022 Maggie Smith

Tree Snow Globe

Design size: 40 x 47 stitches

Use 2 strands of thread for cross stitch

N	Symbol		Number	Name	Stitches
1	□	□	DMC B5200	Snow White	176
2	●	●	DMC 3890	Bright Turquoise - Very Light	237
3	∠	∠	DMC BLANK	White	102
4	◺	◺	DMC 162	Baby Blue - Light	178
5	%	%	DMC 300	Mahogany - Very Dark	107
6	<	<	DMC 307	Lemon	2
7	╳	╳	DMC 434	Brown - Light	33
8	┏	┏	DMC 550	Violet - Very Dark	4
9	✳	✳	DMC 666	Red - Bright	4
10	//	//	DMC 741	Tangerine - Medium	16
11	(	(	DMC 742	Tangerine - Light	88
12	♡	♡	DMC 747	Sky Blue - Very Light	89
13	7	7	DMC 906	Parrot Green - Medium	111
14	m	m	DMC 964	Seagreen - Light	80
15	∘	∘	DMC 972	Canary - Deep	67
16	○	○	DMC 975	Golden Brown - Dark	49
17	♣	♣	DMC 3753	Antique Blue - Ultra Very Light	199
18	#	#	DMC 3843	Electric Blue	4

©2022 Maggie Smith

©2022 Maggie Smith

Trees Snow Globe

Design size: 40 x 47 stitches

Use 2 strands of thread for cross stitch

N	Symbol	Number	Name	Stitches
1	□	DMC B5200	Snow White	90
2	●	DMC 3890	Bright Turquoise - Very Light	237
3	∠	DMC BLANK	White	20
4	◺	DMC 162	Baby Blue - Light	123
5	☆	DMC 300	Mahogany - Very Dark	122
6	<	DMC 550	Violet - Very Dark	16
7	#	DMC 666	Red - Bright	10
8	7	DMC 741	Tangerine - Medium	42
9	X	DMC 742	Tangerine - Light	149
10	♡	DMC 747	Sky Blue - Very Light	83
11	✳	DMC 905	Parrot Green - Dark	128
12	┏	DMC 936	Avocado Green - Very Dark	238
13	m	DMC 964	Seagreen - Light	71
14	▽	DMC 975	Golden Brown - Dark	85
15	♣	DMC 3753	Antique Blue - Ultra Very Light	114
16	■	DMC 3821	Straw	10
17	○	DMC 3885	Blue - Medium Very Dark	8

©2022 Maggie Smith

©2022 Maggie Smith

Peppermint Candy

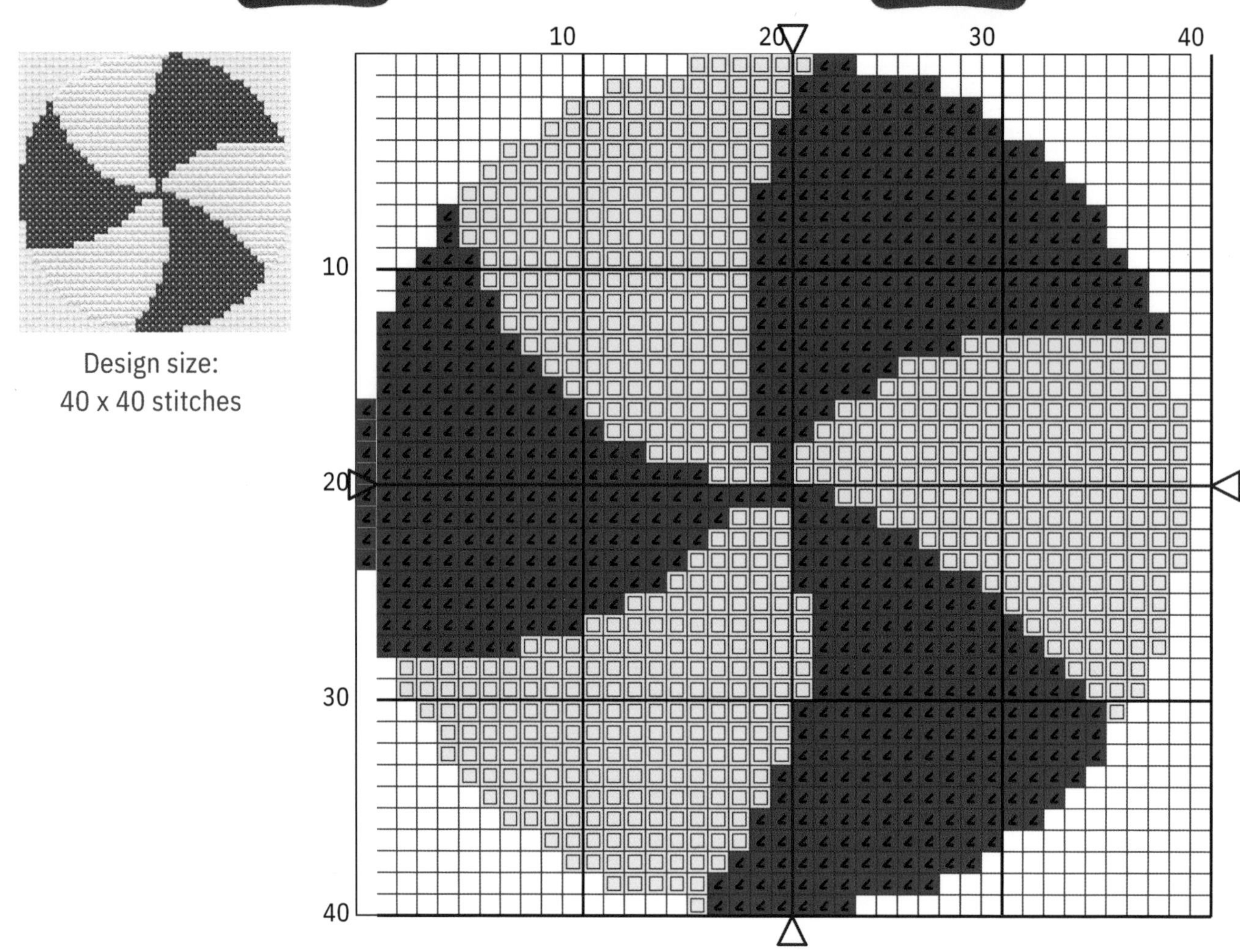

Design size:
40 x 40 stitches

Use 2 strands of thread for cross stitch

N	Symbol		Number	Name	Stitches
1	∠	∠	DMC 349	Coral - Dark	639
2	□	□	DMC 3753	Antique Blue - Ultra Very Light	624

©2022 Maggie Smith

Pie

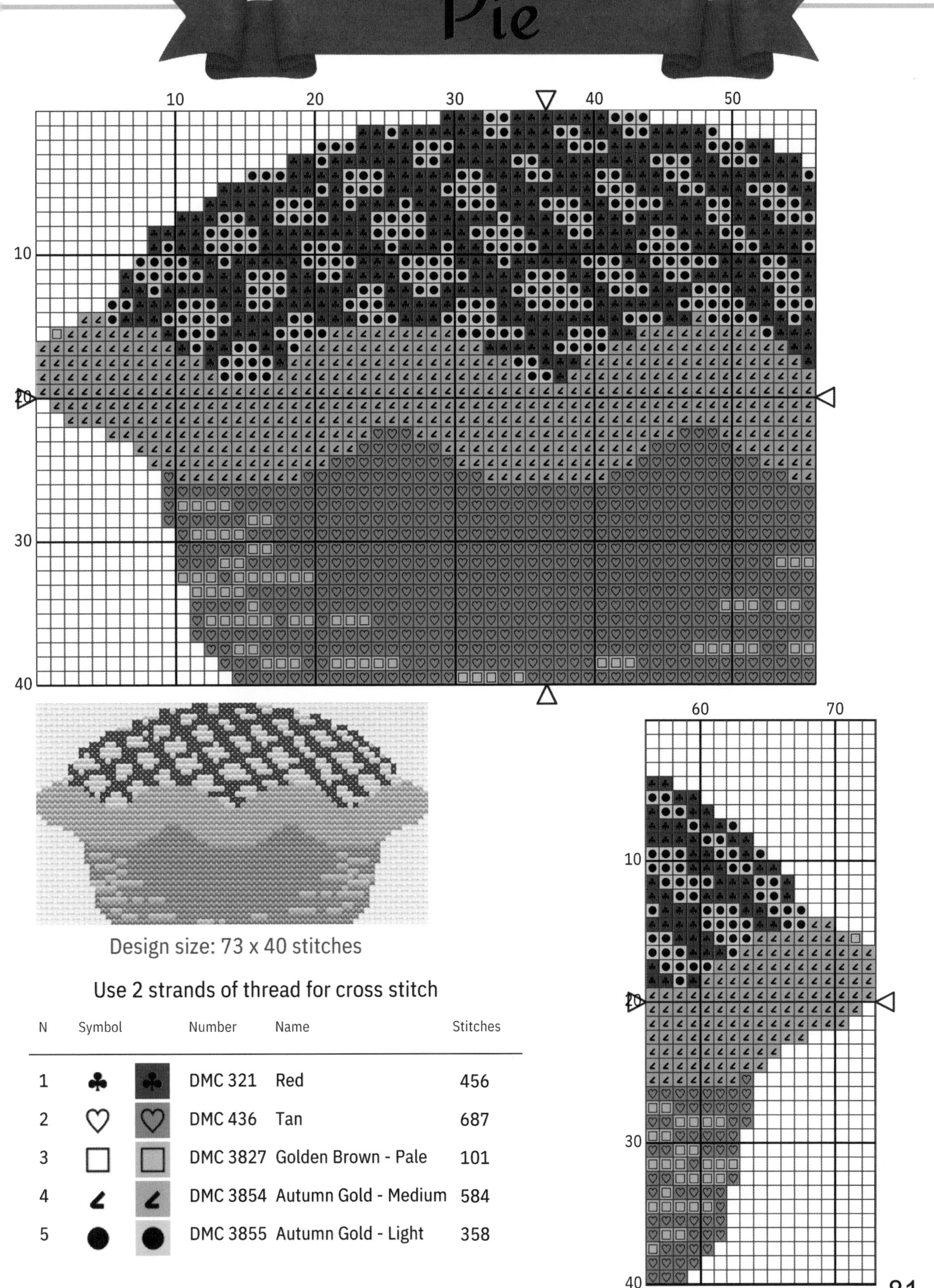

Design size: 73 x 40 stitches

Use 2 strands of thread for cross stitch

N	Symbol	Number	Name	Stitches
1	♣	DMC 321	Red	456
2	♡	DMC 436	Tan	687
3	□	DMC 3827	Golden Brown - Pale	101
4	∠	DMC 3854	Autumn Gold - Medium	584
5	●	DMC 3855	Autumn Gold - Light	358

©2022 Maggie Smith

Candy Cane

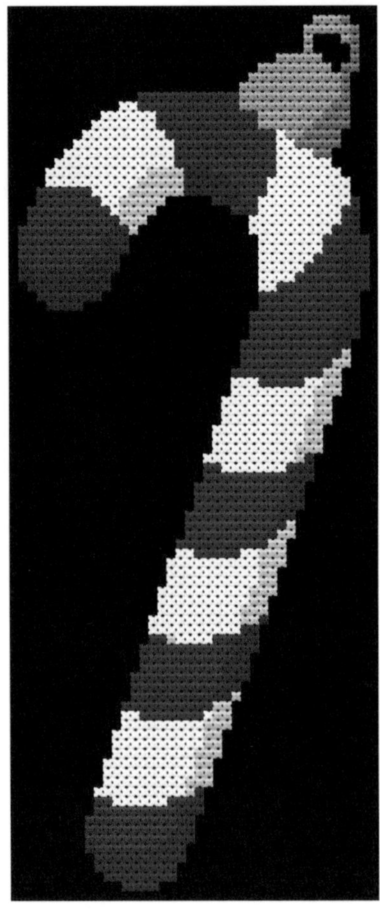

Design size: 40 x 94 stitches

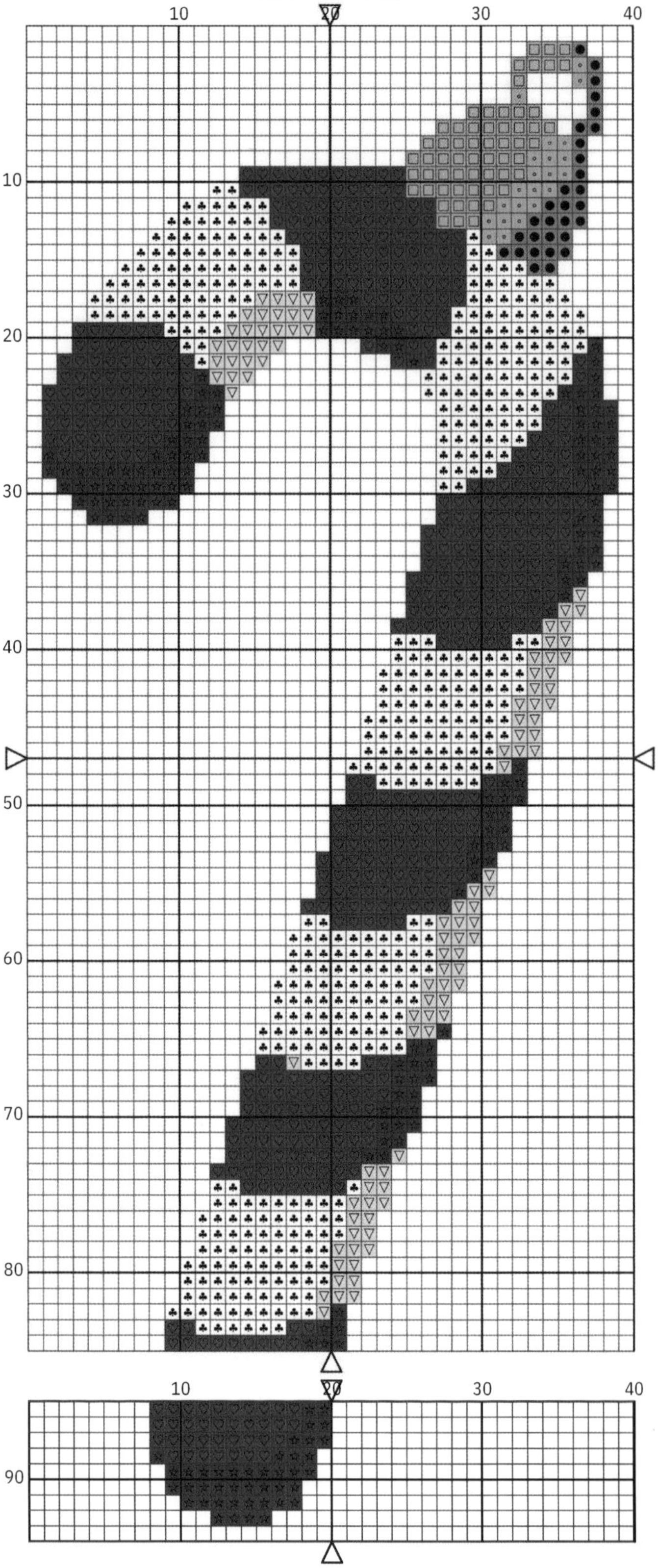

Use 2 strands of thread for cross stitch

N	Symbol	Number	Name	Stitches
1	♡	DMC 349	Coral - Dark	512
2	●	DMC 680	Old Gold - Dark	30
3	□	DMC 972	Canary - Deep	59
4	♣	DMC B5200	Snow White	457
5	▽	DMC 23	Apple Blossom	102
6	∘	DMC 728	Golden Yellow	22
7	☆	DMC 817	Coral Red - Very Dark	187

©2022 Maggie Smith

Old World - Caps

©2022 Maggie Smith

Old World - Lower

©2022 Maggie Smith

Classic Small Letters

©2022 Maggie Smith

Tis the Season Letters

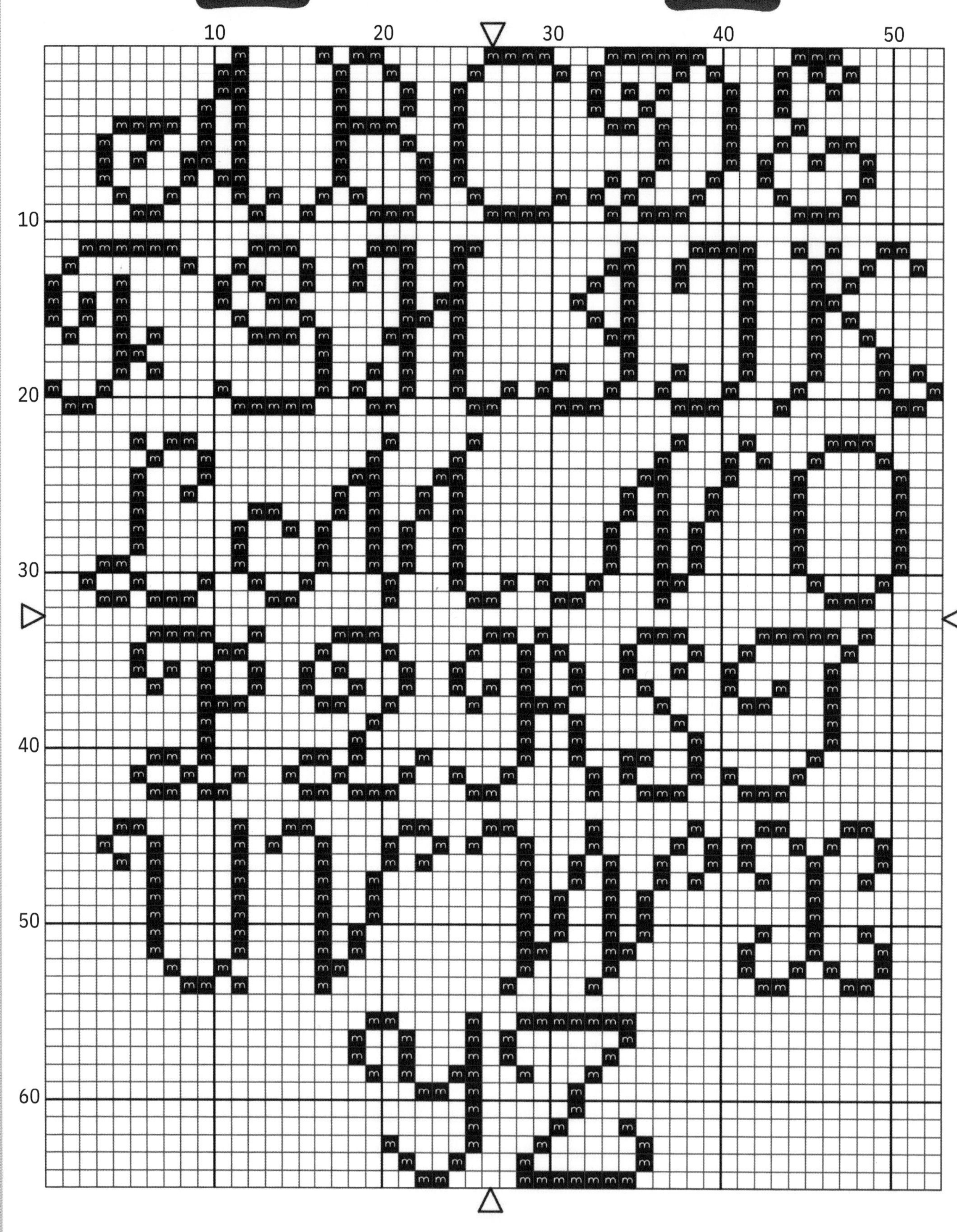

©2022 Maggie Smith

Snowflakes 1

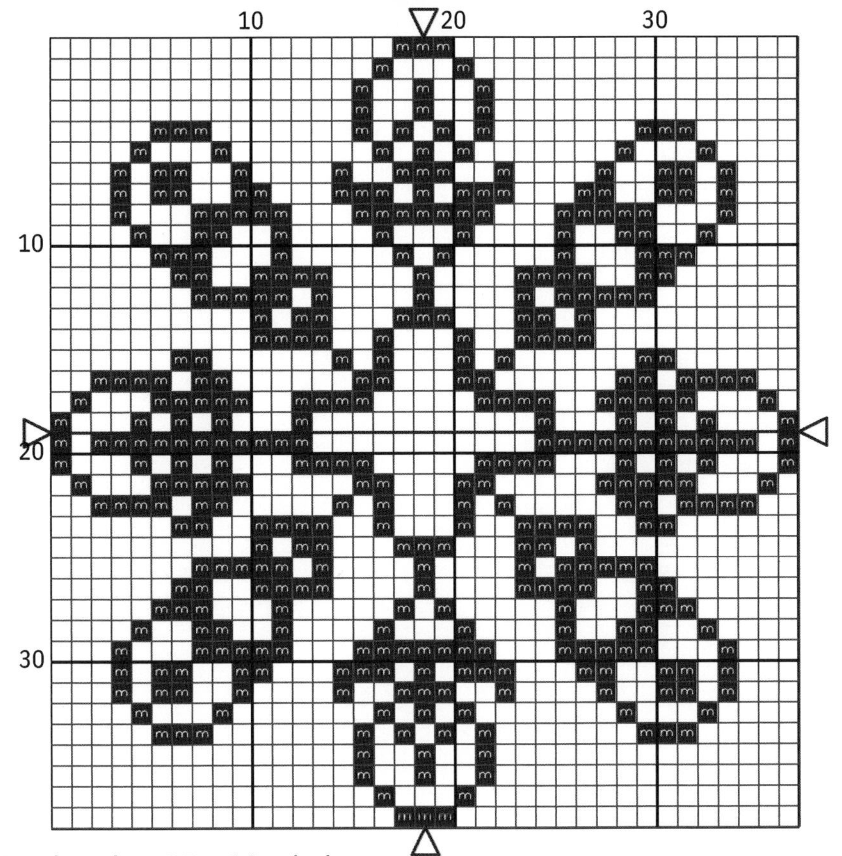

Design size: 37 x 38 stitches

Design size: 35 x 35 stitches

Use 2 strands of thread for cross stitch

©2022 Maggie Smith

Snowflakes 2

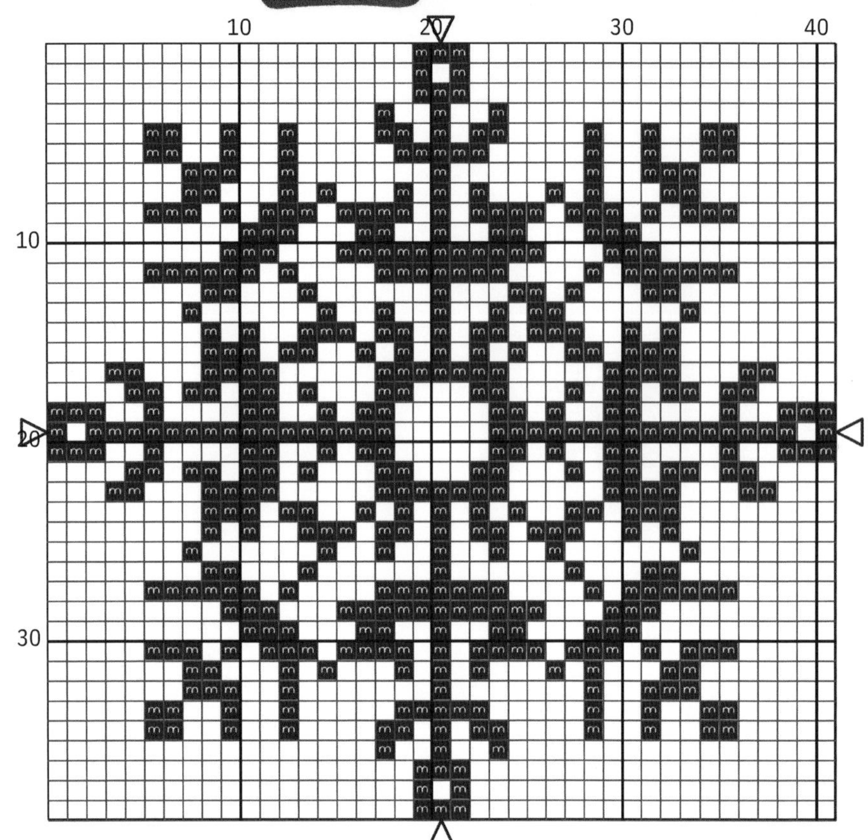

Design size: 41 x 39 stitches

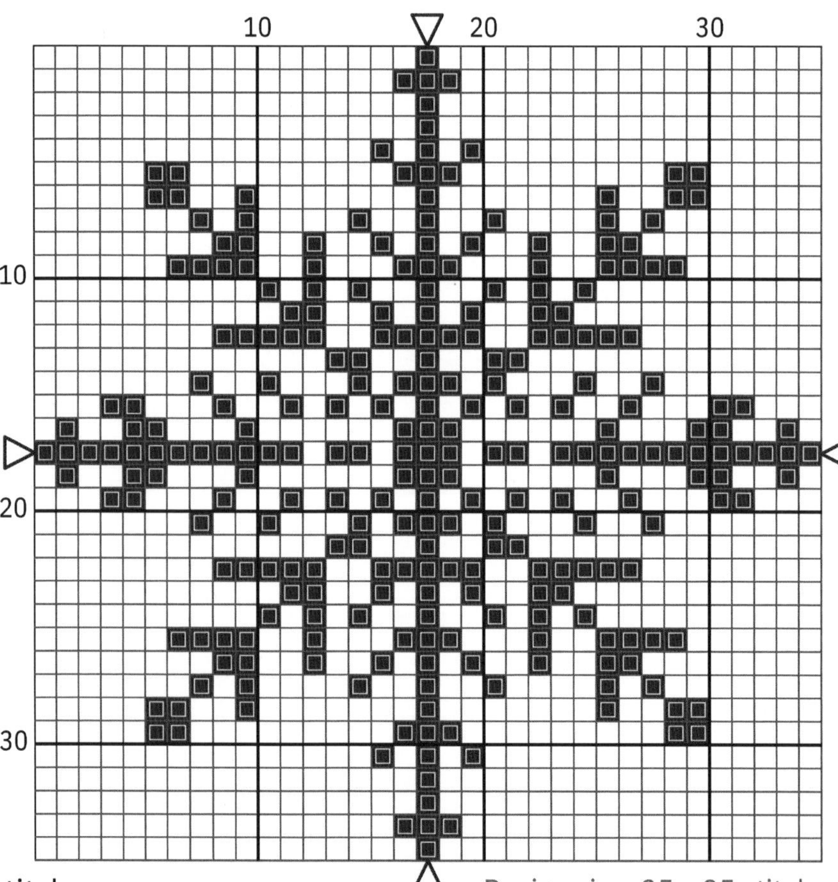

Design size: 35 x 35 stitches

Use 2 strands of thread for cross stitch

©2022 Maggie Smith

Snowflakes 3

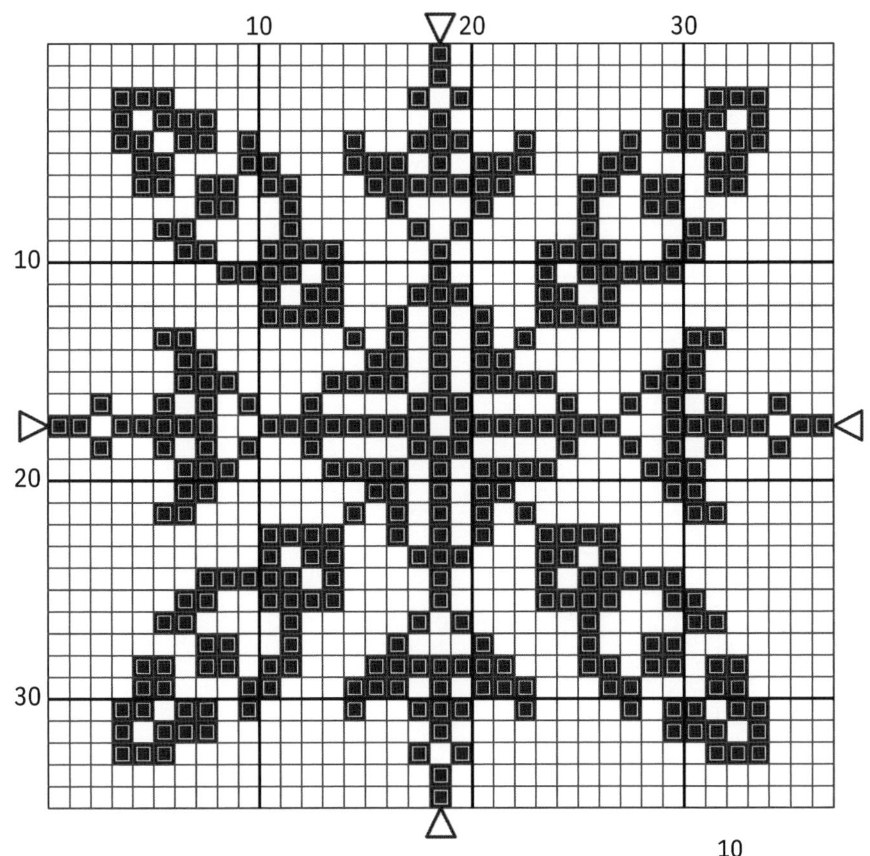

Design size: 37 x 35 stitches

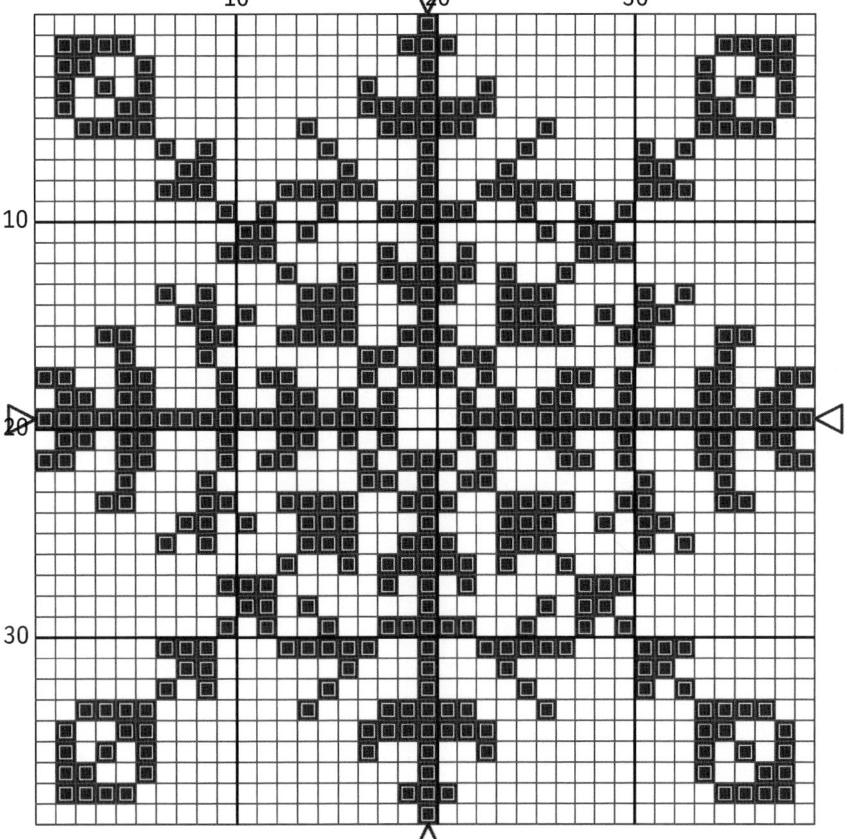

Design size: 39 x 39 stitches

Use 2 strands of thread for cross stitch

©2022 Maggie Smith

Snowflakes 4

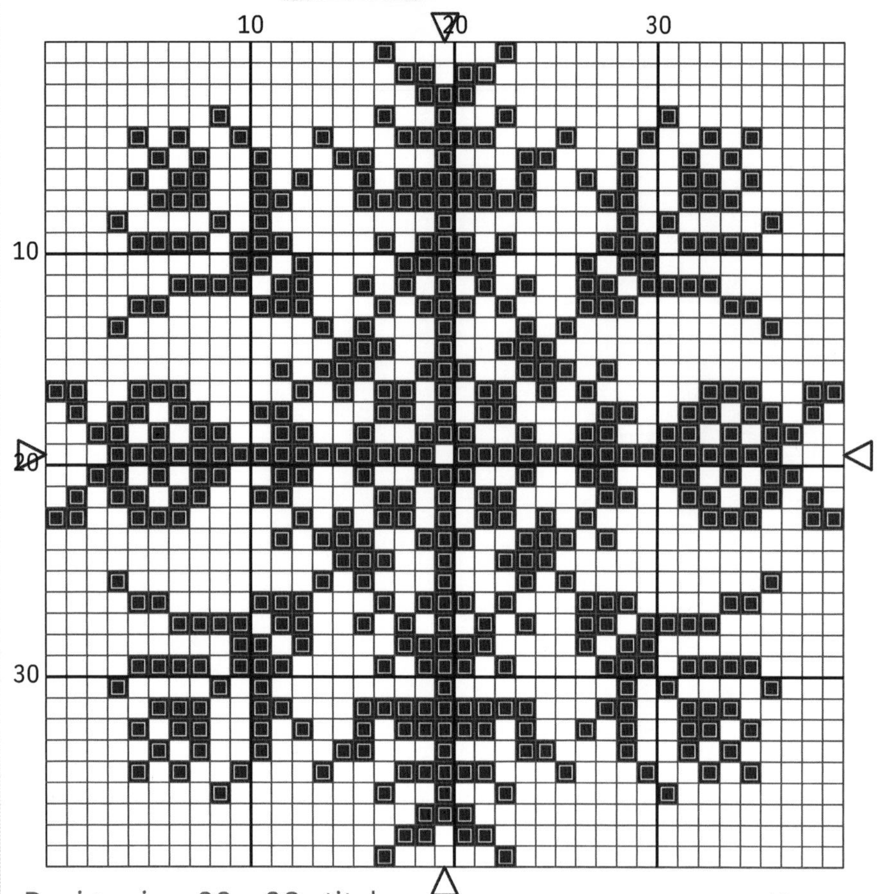

Design size: 39 x 39 stitches

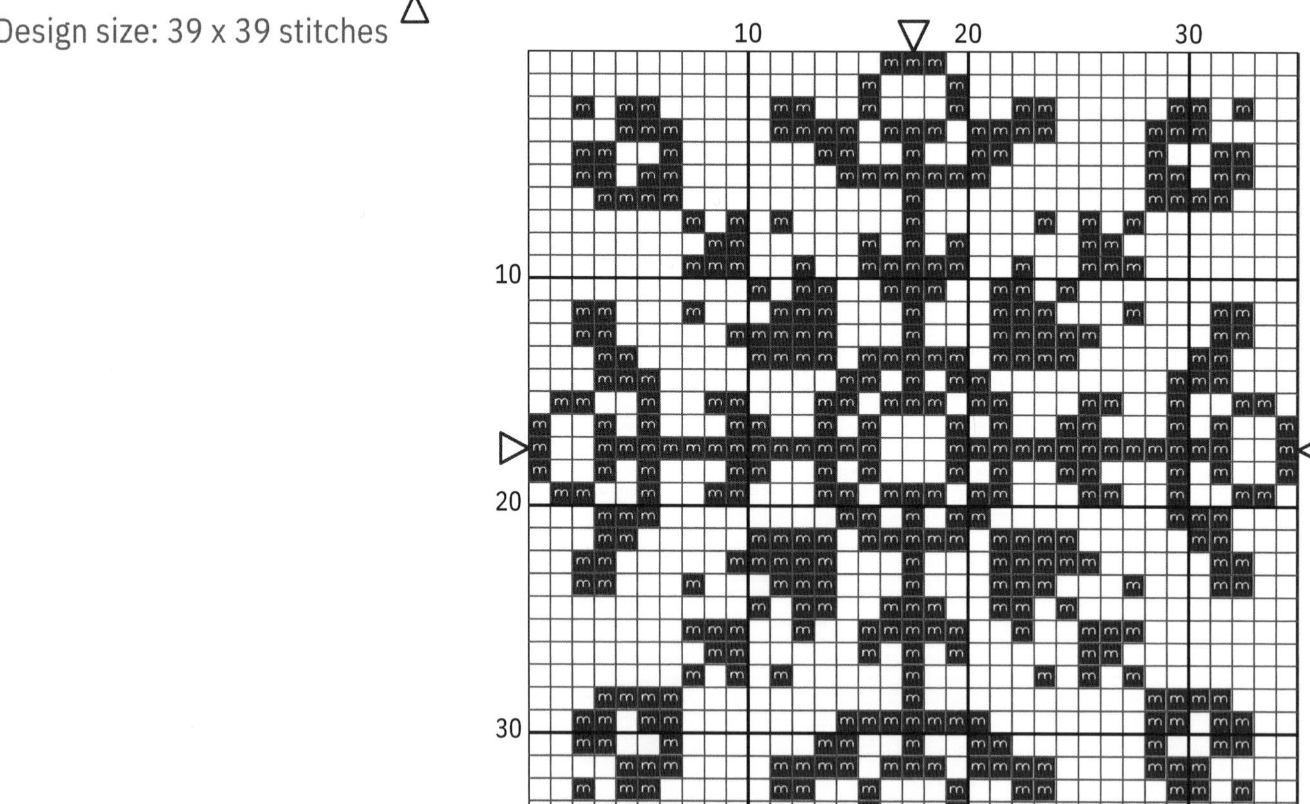

Design size: 35 x 35 stitches

Use 2 strands of thread for cross stitch

©2022 Maggie Smith

Mini Sampler

Design size: 55 x 55 stitches

Use 2 strands of thread for cross stitch

N	Symbol		Number	Name	Stitches
1	m	m	DMC 310	Black	1139

©2022 Maggie Smith

Mini Sampler 2

Design size: 55 x 55 stitches

Use 2 strands of thread for cross stitch

N	Symbol		Number	Name	Stitches
1	०	■	DMC 310	Black	1137

©2022 Maggie Smith

Mini Sampler 3

Design size: 55 x 55 stitches

Use 2 strands of thread for cross stitch

N	Symbol		Number	Name	Stitches
1	m	m	DMC 310	Black	1090

©2022 Maggie Smith

Borders 1

Borders 2

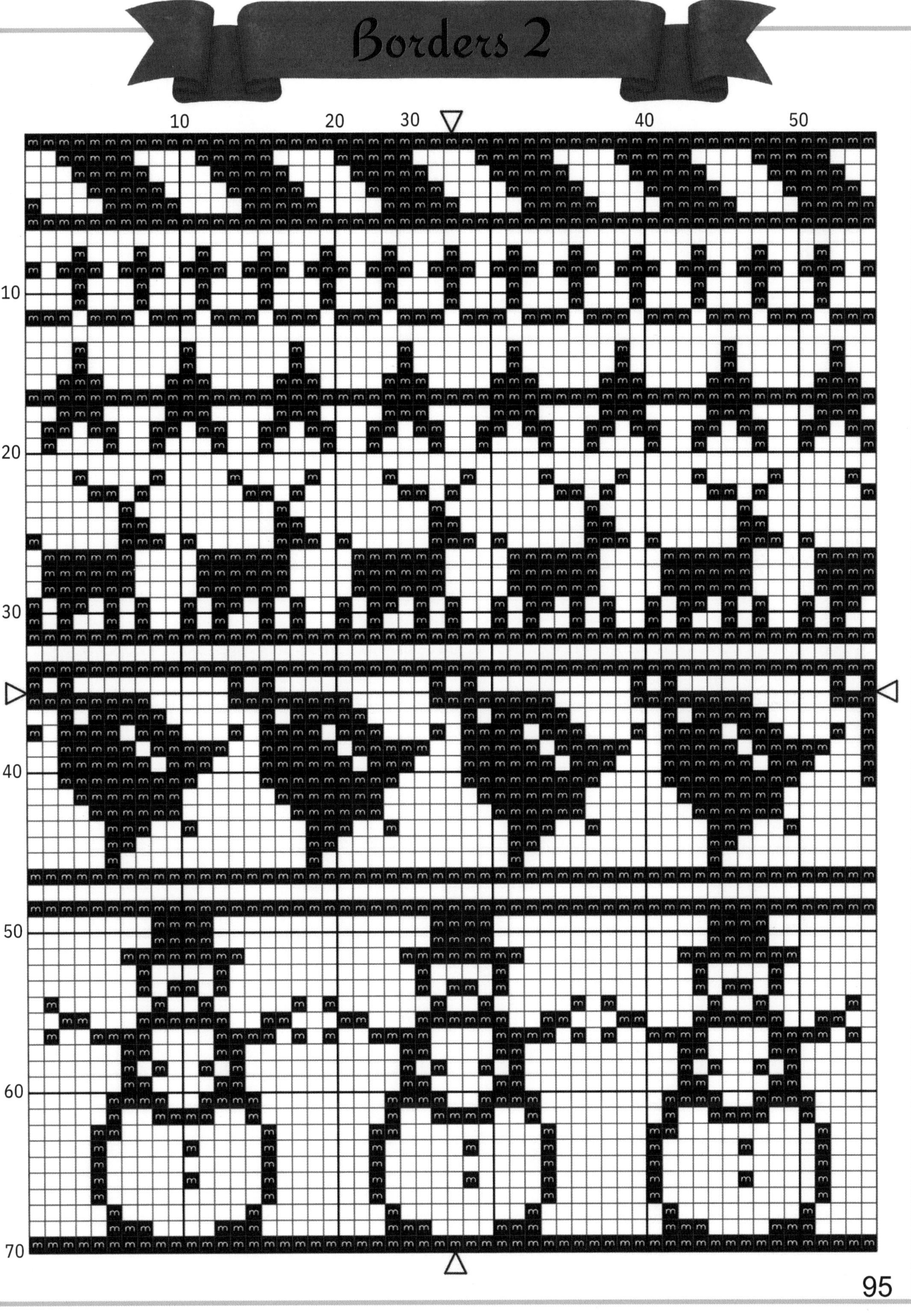

Borders 3

Borders 4

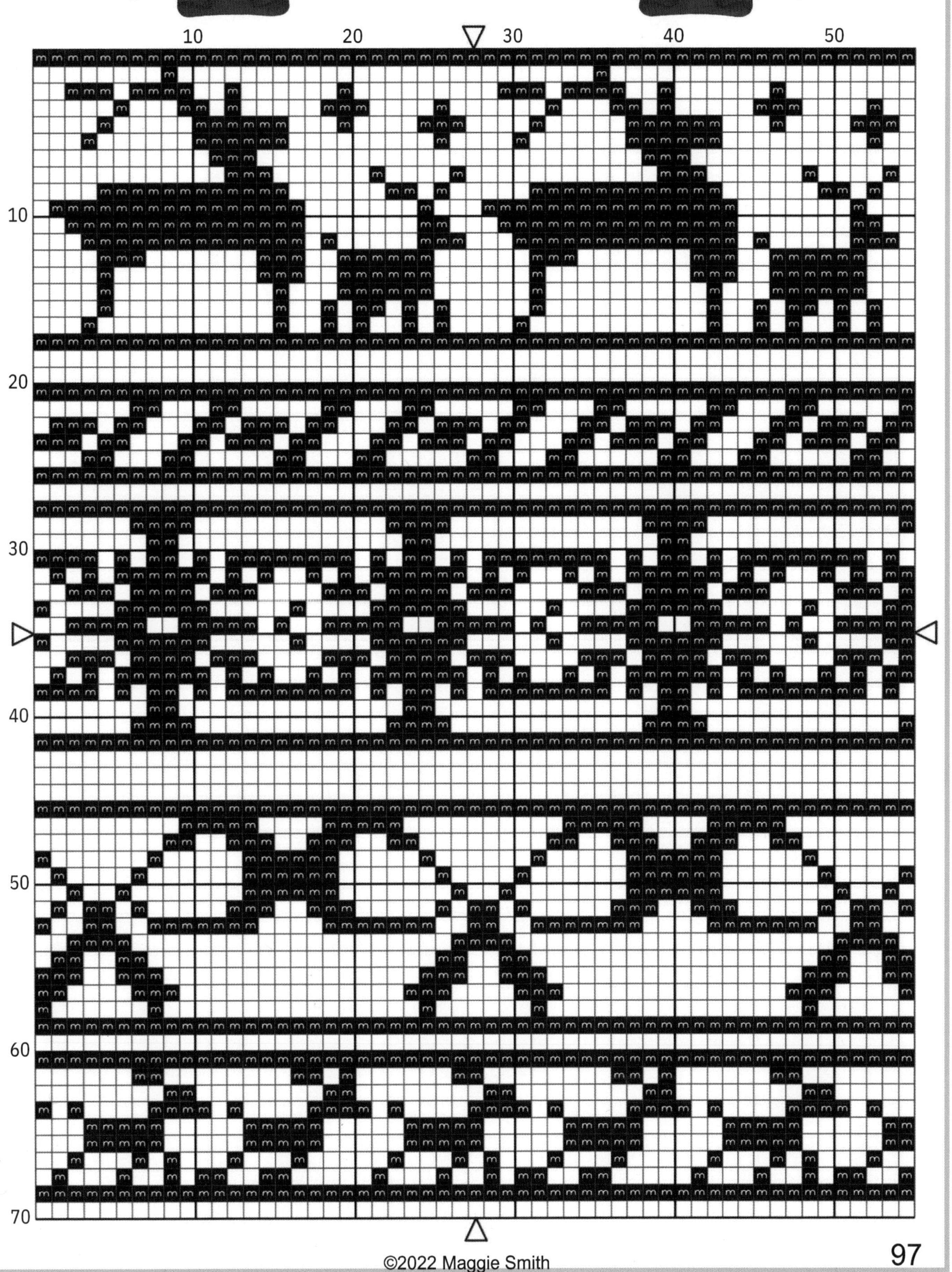

©2022 Maggie Smith

Printed in Great Britain
by Amazon